FOR THE LOVE OF PICKLES

Left to right: Pickled Collins (pg. 142) Pickled Bourbon Sour (pg. 143), Jalapeño Pickle Margarita (pg. 135)

FOR THE LOVE OF PICKLES

Easy-to-Make Food and Drink Recipes with Every Part of the Pickle

SCOTT KAYLIN

Foreword by J. B. Smoove

Photography by Eddie Sanchez

Andrews McMeel
PUBLISHING®

I would like to dedicate this book to my family, who fill my life with love and laughter. Nothing brings us greater joy than being in the kitchen together, creating and sharing amazing food and drinks.

CONTENTS

FOREWORD
BY J. B. SMOOVE

Hey, food enthusiast, it's J. B. Smoove here, and I'm thrilled to introduce you to a culinary gem brought to you by Scott Kaylin, aka the Pickle Man! You know it's always good to have a "guy" for things, like your "plumbing guy" or your "car guy." Well, Scott is our pickle guy, and my wife, Shah, and I are loyal customers. Honestly, I got into the pickle game a little late: my bride got me in it, and it was Scott who kept me in it.

It doesn't matter—sweet, hot 'n' spicy, savory, garlic, and kosher dill—there are so many, and I find them all delicious! Their flavor grabs your taste buds and won't let go! So when Scott asked me to write a foreword for his book, I said, "Scott, what's wrong with you?!? Don't you realize this isn't just any cookbook? You could pickle the books and sell them in a jar. You could sign the jars, and people would love it! That's how good you are at pickling!" He said, "Maybe the next one," and while that may sound like a polite no, I still think it's a great idea . . . but I digress.

Look, this damn book is a journey into the intricate and tangy world of pickles, where you can elevate meals with one of nature's greatest gifts! My wife is passionate about pickles—"pickle passion," some would say—and Scott showed us that a pickle can be enjoyed in the afternoon while wearing shorts and a T-shirt, snacking on fried pickle slices on the couch, or nibbling on quarter slices at an elegant evening event while dressed to the nines! Scott is able to take something as simple as a pickle and transform it into a star. Simply put, Scott is a damn show-off!

You know, when we met Scott, we instantly saw his passion for what he does! As a matter of fact, when he hugs you, he gives off (in a good way) the slight scent of pickle. What that does is make you want a damn pickle; I think that's an old pickler's trick. Oh, and if you know anything about the pickling process, it takes time and patience! I looked it up and saw that it could take anywhere from five to twenty-one days. . . . That's dedication, and that's Scott, a dedicated damn pickler! So whether you're a kitchen newbie or a culinary connoisseur, these recipes are designed to inspire creativity and bring joy to your table. Trust me. As a man who has been told he looks slightly like a chocolate-covered pickle, after you dive into this book, you'll be seeing pickles in a whole new light. Get ready to embark on a flavor-packed adventure filled with laughter, deliciousness, and unforgettable moments. Grab your apron, and let's create amazing dishes on our way to greatness with Scott Kaylin at the helm. Thank me later!

CLASSIC DILL
KAYLIN+KAYLIN PICKLES
KOSHER DILL
KAYLIN+KAYLIN PICKLES
SPICY DILL CHIPS
KAYLIN+KAYLIN PICKLES
HORSERADISH
SPICY GARLIC SPEARS
KAYLIN + KAYLIN PICKLES
BLAZING SOUR
FULL SOUR
KAYLIN+KAYLIN PICKLES
HALF SOUR
JALAPENO
KAYLIN+KAYLIN PICKLES
SWEET HEAT CHIPS
KAYLIN+KAYLIN PICKLES
HONEY MUSTARD CHIPS
BREAD N' BUTTER CHIPS

INTRODUCTION

WELCOME TO HAPPINESS IN EVERY CRUNCH

MY HISTORY

I didn't set out to become the Pickle Man. But here we are—and here's how it happened.

I grew up in New York, where pickles were everywhere. At the deli, at the bodega, next to your sandwich, on your sandwich, or attached to a stick from a street cart. You didn't have to ask for them. You didn't have to think about them. Good pickles just showed up . . . everywhere.

I never realized how much that mattered to me until decades later when my wife and I moved to Vancouver, British Columbia. Suddenly, good pickles were gone. No bodega pickles. No hoagie-sized pickles to hold like Popsicles. No decent pickle platters at the deli. Vancouver, it turned out, was a pickle desert. Gone were the days when I snapped into a world-class dill without thought.

What started as a craving turned into something much bigger. I didn't just miss the flavor—I missed the ritual, the crunch, the comfort I hadn't even realized was built into every bite. And as a lifelong entrepreneur, that familiar itch kicked in: there's a gap—let's fill it. However, there was just one tiny, inconsequential hiccup . . . I had no idea how to make a pickle! Whoops!

So I did what any determined, slightly obsessive pickle-lover would do. I went back to New York and scoured the annual Picklefest to find a pickler to make ME into *the* Pickle Man. I shook hands with young picklers, middle-aged picklers like me, and old-school pickle families, hoping to meet *the one* who could help me bring good pickles to the West Coast. Eventually, I partnered with a third-generation pickler who helped create not only a classically crunchy, beautifully briny dill but also wild flavors that would intrigue the pickle-curious. These pickles were kind of a big deal. Back in Vancouver,

I opened at Granville Island Public Market and sold out in six days. As it turns out, the people of Vancouver really needed a good pickle.

A few years later, we moved to Los Angeles, and I opened a pickle tasting bar at the Original Farmers Market. It was early 2020, and my stall was (and still is!) surrounded by butchers, cheesemongers, rotisserie spinners, tea brewers, and—crucially—a beer tap. Cold pints met salty cravings just steps away from each other. I handed out samples that turned into sales, sales into regulars, and regulars into lines. I put on a bow tie. *The* Pickle Man was born.

But like so many stories from that year, everything changed with COVID, and I was caught in a pickle. The market emptied. Only "essential" vendors could stay—and pickles, sadly, didn't make the cut. I wasn't ready to quit, though, so I called the health department and made my case: pickles come from cucumbers, cucumbers are vegetables—so pickles are essential. They laughed. I pushed. They agreed. The Pickle Man lived to pickle another day!

Many things led to many other things (like me . . . ME! . . . going viral on TikTok), and now I run two stalls at the market. Kaylin + Kaylin is a place for your classic and wildly flavored pickles. The other is Topped, akin to a scoop shop, where adventurous taste buds choose wild toppings to fill scooped-out pickles or pile onto chips. A hollowed-out dill smothered with Nutella? Don't knock it till you try it (see page 84 and report back). We also ship nationwide, so no matter where you are, we're just one click away.

Which brings me to this book, a love letter to flavor—and to fun. Inside, you'll find breakfasts, snacks, cocktails, desserts, and party tricks that let pickles play both the sidekick and the star.

Whether you're here for the crunch, the tradition, the nostalgia, or just a good laugh inspired by a "Wow, that's a new flavor" moment—I'm glad you made it.

These recipes are created with pickles and some of my pals, chefs I know, and other fun surprises from contributors across the country.

This book is a pickle playground! Go on. Have fun.

PICKLE HISTORY

Pickles have been around longer than sliced bread—literally. While the first bread-slicing machine showed up in 1928, pickles go all the way back to around 2400 BCE, when clever Mesopotamians started soaking cucumbers in salty brine to keep them fresh for long journeys and cold winters. The cucumbers themselves? They came from India, traveling along ancient trade routes before taking their briny plunge in Mesopotamia.

By 2030 BCE, pickling had already taken root in the Tigris Valley, and by 850 BCE, Aristotle was praising cucumbers for their healing powers. Roman emperors like Julius Caesar fed pickles to their troops for strength and stamina—a tradition that oddly resurfaced in 2000, when the Philadelphia Eagles credited their blowout win over the Cowboys to chugging pickle juice in the scorching heat. "I may start drinking pickle juice when I'm just sitting home chilling," said defensive end Hugh Douglas.

And rumor has it that Cleopatra credited pickles as part of her beauty regimen. I get that, Cleopatra. I get that.

By the Middle Ages, pickles were a staple in English pantries. Queen Elizabeth I was a fan, and even Shakespeare was throwing shade with pickle metaphors—"How now, sot?!" (basically the 1600s version of "What in the brine?"). As global exploration ramped up in the fifteenth and sixteenth centuries, pickles became standard issue for sailors, who relied on their briny bite to fend off scurvy—long before limes (or gin and tonics) took over the job.

By 1659, Dutch farmers in what is now Brooklyn were growing cucumbers and selling pickled versions on New York's bustling market streets. If you've ever had a classic New York deli pickle, you're tasting that legacy. Then in the late nineteenth and early twentieth centuries, Jewish immigrants from eastern Europe arrived with their own pickle traditions—most famously, the kosher dill: garlicky, fermented, and unapologetically sour. The Lower East Side became a pickle paradise, with barrels lining the sidewalks and the sharp scent of brine drifting through tenement kitchens.

Meanwhile, a guy named Steven Trotter became the youngest man to conquer the crest of Niagara Falls . . . in two plastic pickle barrels tied together with rubber inner tubes.

>10,000 BCE
500 BCE
800 CE
1800s
1940s
1950s
1960s

PICKLES
1970s
1980s
1990s
2000s

Pickles are for everyone—every age, every background. I've had people tell me about feeding their baby a pickle for the first time and watching them scrunch their face . . . then go back in for another bite. Which, incidentally, was also my experience with pickles and Nutella. I've catered weddings with full-blown pickle bars. I've watched three generations share a pickle flight and argue (lovingly) over which flavor wins. (It's always Honey Mustard. Sweet Heat. Unless it's Horseradish.)

Pickles bring people together. They always have.

And sure, not everyone's a fan. But the beauty of pickles is this: for every person who passes, someone nearby will happily take theirs. It always works out.

TYPES OF PICKLES

SHAPES AND SIZES

Pickles come in all shapes and sizes—and for this book, you can use any of them. Most recipes call for them to be chopped, diced, or blended, anyway, so don't stress about using the "right" one if you don't have it. Use what you've got.

Chips

Classic, round, waffle-cut slices with ridges—perfect for burgers, sandwiches, or piling onto just about anything. Their cut maximizes surface area and delivers extra crunch. You can use them *on* things or *as* things, like in place of tortilla chips for a take on nachos (see page 53).

Spears

Long wedges usually quartered lengthwise. Great for snacking straight out of the jar or tucking into a sandwich for a satisfying bite. This is the one your pickle-averse friend will push to the side of the plate while you stare at it the whole meal waiting for the moment to ask, "Can I have your pickle?"

Whole

The full cucumber, pickled in all its glory. Great for pickle purists who like to walk and pickle down a busy city street or waiting in the Peter Pan line at Disneyland. These are also wonderful for scooping out and making into a vessel to fill with liquids or other fun things. You can even replace bread with halved wholes and make a pickle sandwich.

Stackers (Long Slices)

Thin, lengthwise slices that lie flat—perfect for layering in sandwiches and on burgers when you want full coverage and minimal slippage. You can even slap your friends with these. Whack!

Relish

Chopped fine. Sweet or spicy—great in salads, on hot dogs, or stirred into mayo-based dressings and dips.

Mini (Cornichon Style)

Small, snackable, textured, and easy for nibbling. Great on charcuterie boards or for when you want just a quick hit.

FLAVORS

Classic Dill

This is your no-frills, straight-shooting pickle. It has a clean and sharp taste with dill leading the way. The flavor is fresh and balanced—salty, slightly sour, and lightly herbal without being overpowering. This is the traditional pickle most people picture when they think of a classic spear.

Kosher Dill

Kosher Dill pickles are a bolder, more intensely flavored version of the Classic Dill. They're inspired by traditional Jewish deli-style pickles and known for their strong garlic presence, pronounced saltiness, and deep, savory brine. The flavor is sharp, tangy, and noticeably more robust, with no sweetness. They're crisp, assertive, and full of character. If Classic Dills are mild and balanced, Kosher Dills bring more punch and personality to the plate.

Bread and Butter

Bread and Butter pickles are sweet and mildly spiced, making them one of the most recognizable—and most debated—pickle varieties. Known for their distinctive balance of sugar and vinegar, they're typically thin sliced and flavored, with spices like mustard seed, onion, and a hint of clove or celery seed.

They're also the most controversial pickle on the plate. For some, that unexpected sweetness is nostalgic and comforting. For others, it's a deal-breaker—especially if they bite in expecting a Classic Dill. Their flavor profile breaks the mold of what people think a pickle *should* be, which is exactly why they spark such strong opinions. Love them or leave them!

Honey Mustard

This one is where sweet meets spicy. I combine the classic brine with honey, mustard, and other spices to give these pickles a mellow sweetness with that signature mustard zip. They've got warm, savory notes that hit your taste buds from every angle. I love watching people try these for the first time. Even pickle haters like these pickles.

Sweet-and-Sour

Sweet-and-sour pickles have a balanced flavor that combines mild sweetness with a noticeable tang. They're neither overly sugary nor aggressively sour, with just enough sugar to soften the vinegar's sharpness.

Horseradish

This one's not for the faint of heart. I use fresh horseradish in the brine for a deep, earthy heat—not just spice but a kind of zippy warmth that rises up and screams, "I'm here!"

Sweet Heat

This is the wild card that became a bestseller. It starts off like a sweet pickle—smooth, familiar, maybe even a little playful—then hits you with a kick that builds slowly and finishes with a warm burn. I balance cinnamon into the brine, which isn't very clear until you know it's there. It's the back note that keeps people trying more and more until they figure it out.

Spicy Garlic Spears

Garlic cloves are dunked into the brine and left to brew alongside these spears to create a multilayered journey of flavor and crunch. The garlic is front and center, and the spice builds with each bite but doesn't overwhelm.

Jalapeño

These pickles are made with thick slices of jalapeños in a simple vinegar brine. They have a bright flavor with the distinct taste (and kick!) of fresh jalapeño—slightly grassy and earthy. The heat is moderate and lingers briefly, so it's not overpowering. They're a good choice if you want a pickle with a little spice and strong pepper flavor.

BRINED PICKLES

What Is Brining?

Brining is the age-old technique of preserving food by soaking it in a salty, acidic solution—and it's the backbone of nearly every pickle in this book.

The version most people know today is the quick brine: a vinegar-based method where cucumbers (or other vegetables) are soaked in a mixture of vinegar, water, salt, and spices. It doesn't rely on fermentation or weeks-long preservation time. Instead, it delivers that crisp, sour, bright-tasting pickle you know and love—fast. That's what you'll find in most grocery store jars, and it's what we use at Kaylin + Kaylin to create bold, consistent flavor in every batch.

Nearly every culture has developed its own version—brining everything from fish to lemons to cabbage. Why has it stuck around? Because it works. Brining preserves food, enhances flavor, adds acidity, and brings a sharp brightness that wakes up anything it touches. In this book, you'll use brine to punch up sauces, marinades, salad dressings, cocktails, dips—even desserts.

We treat brine like liquid gold. Don't toss it—taste it, cook with it, chug it, and let it surprise you.

Here's how it works:

1. Cucumbers are packed into jars—either whole, halved, speared, or sliced.
2. A hot or cold brine is poured over them. That brine is made from:
   - Vinegar (usually distilled white, apple cider, or rice vinegar)
   - Water (to dilute the acidity)
   - Salt (for flavor and preservation)
   - Sugar (optional, for balance)
   - Spices, garlic, herbs, and aromatics
3. The cucumbers soak in that brine for anywhere from a few hours (for quick pickles) to one or two weeks (for deep flavor).

What's happening:

- The acetic acid in vinegar acts fast, penetrating the cucumber's cells and acidifying the entire environment.
- This low pH (around 2.5–4.0) kills off spoilage organisms and preserves the cucumbers.
- Salt helps draw out moisture via osmosis, firming the texture and infusing flavor.
- Spices and aromatics steep into the flesh, creating bold, punchy flavors.

FERMENTED PICKLES

What Is Fermenting?

Fermentation is the slower, living cousin of brining—and it skips the vinegar entirely.

Instead of pouring in acid, you let natural microbes create it for you. Salt draws out water from the cucumbers (or whatever you're fermenting), and that salty environment invites good bacteria to move in and get to work. Over time, they convert sugars into lactic acid, which preserves the food and creates that signature fermented flavor.

The result? A complex, deeply flavorful pickle with probiotic benefits and a living brine. Every batch has its own personality, shaped by time, temperature, and the natural microbes doing their thing. It's funkier. More nuanced.

Here's how it works:

1. Cucumbers are submerged in a saltwater brine (no vinegar).
2. That brine usually contains:
   - Non-iodized salt (like kosher or sea salt)
   - Filtered water (chlorine-free, to avoid killing bacteria)
   - Optional: garlic, dill, peppercorns, grape leaves (which help with crunch)
3. The cucumbers sit at room temperature in this brine for several days to several weeks.

What's happening:

- Naturally occurring lactic acid bacteria—like *Lactobacillus plantarum*—live on the surface of cucumbers.
- In the salty, oxygen-poor brine, they outcompete harmful microbes and start feeding on the natural sugars in the cucumbers.
- As they digest these sugars, they produce lactic acid, which gradually lowers the pH and preserves the pickles.
- Along the way, they also create gases (like CO_2), flavor compounds, and beneficial enzymes.

Texture and color changes:

- The cucumbers lose chlorophyll and turn a duller green.
- The skin becomes more tender and flexible.
- The brine may become cloudy—a good sign! It means the microbes are doing their job.
- You'll get some bubbling or fizzing, especially early on.

FLAVORS

New Pickle

These are barely pickled at all. I give them just enough time in the brine to start the transformation—maybe one or two days. The result? Crunchy, refreshing, and still basically a cucumber but with the early signs of something more. These are what you reach for when you want the vibe of a pickle but the freshness of something just off the vine.

Half Sour

Half sours are fermented for a little longer than new pickles, so they keep more of their cucumber flavor and bright-green color. A little salty, super crisp, and very snackable. They're a gateway pickle: perfect for someone new to fermented flavors.

Full Sour

These cucumbers have gone all the way. They've been in the brine long enough to lose most of their original sweetness and pick up a deep . . . funk. They're bold, cloudy, soft but still snappy, and unapologetically sour. Old-school deli energy.

Blazing Sour

This is the full sour's spicy cousin. Same long fermentation, same depth, but with heat. I add fresh chili and garlic during fermentation to give the natural tang an extra layer of kick. These aren't just sour—they're *alive*. You'll feel them in your chest like after slurping a level-five curry.

SAUERKRAUT

Sauerkraut is humble cabbage transformed through fermentation. Made by combining shredded cabbage with salt and letting it sit, sauerkraut relies on naturally occurring lactic acid bacteria to kick off a slow metamorphosis. Over the course of one to several weeks, those microbes turn the cabbage's sugars into lactic acid, preserving it and giving it that signature sour bite. The result is a crisp, craveable condiment packed with gut-friendly probiotics and depth of flavor. It's been a staple across cultures for centuries—from German bratwurst stands to Reuben sandwiches . . . and now fun-filled dishes throughout this book.

HOW TO USE THIS BOOK

This isn't a rigid, rules-based cookbook. It's an inspiration for all the wondrous things you can do with pickles.

You'll find recipes that call for actual pickles—sliced, chopped, blitzed, or stacked—and others that use pickle brine as a flavor booster, a secret weapon, or the star of the show.

But here's the thing: aside from desserts (which are a little more precise), the number of pickles you use is totally up to you. Think of them like hot sauce or chili flakes: Want extra zing? Add more. Prefer subtle? Go light. Pickles are flexible. Use what you love, skip what you don't, and taste as you go.

You'll also see specific brine flavors mentioned—Sweet Heat, Horseradish, Honey Mustard, and others. Those are great if you've got them, but brines are interchangeable. Don't have what's listed? Use a classic kosher dill or whatever jar is in your fridge. It all works; just go with what's on hand and trust your taste buds. Also, most recipes will work with refrigerated or shelf-stable pickles.

And don't worry—this book isn't just for pickle obsessives. Even if your dining companions aren't the type to eat pickles straight from the jar, they'll still find plenty to love. In many recipes, pickles aren't the main event; they're an accent. A layer of brightness, acidity, or crunch that brings everything else to life.

RECIPES

PICKLES

BREAKFAST

This chapter is proof that brine belongs at the table long before lunchtime. Pickles might not be your go-to morning ingredient, but that salty, tangy bite is the perfect contrast to rich, savory, and even sweet breakfast staples. Whether they're chopped into Corned Beef Reuben (Sma-)Hashed (page 18), whipped into cream cheese, or layered onto Avocado Toast with Pickles, Sprouts, and Radishes (page 21), pickles wake up your taste buds and cut through the heaviness of the morning.

Think about it: maple syrup loves a little acid to cut through the sweetness—enter the sharp pickle alongside a syrupy Chicken and Waffle Sando (page 22). Brines balance the richness of Pickle-Brined Crispy Breakfast Potatoes and Pickle Milk Biscuits (pages 25 and 29, respectively) and add depth, punch, and just enough surprise to pair perfectly with your morning brew.

CORNED BEEF REUBEN (SMA-)HASHED

Serves 2

This is your go-to deli sandwich reimagined in a skillet. Smashed potatoes mix with corned beef, melty Swiss, and sauerkraut for a dish that's part brunch, part dinner, and just 100% yum. Serve straight from the pan to really make your friends and family ogle at the table.

8–10 small fingerling potatoes
1 teaspoon kosher salt
Extra-virgin olive oil
Freshly ground black pepper
2 tablespoons salted butter
½ cup mustard sauerkraut
8 slices deli corned beef, sliced thick, medium diced
2 ounces Swiss cheese, grated
2 pieces fresh dill, for garnish
2 slices marble rye bread, toasted

Place the potatoes and salt in a medium pot and fill it with enough water to cover the potatoes by 1 inch. Bring to a boil and cook for about 7 minutes, or until the potatoes are soft and fork tender. Drain the potatoes and let them cool slightly. (This step can also be done the night before or earlier in the day before assembly.)

Preheat the oven to broil. On the stove, heat a large cast-iron skillet over medium-high heat. Add enough olive oil to generously cover the bottom of the pan by about 1 tablespoon and add the potatoes.

Oil the bottom of a smaller oven-proof skillet and use it to smash down the potatoes to about ¼ inch thick. Sear one side then flip and sear the other until they are golden brown and season generously with salt and pepper to taste. Meanwhile, line a plate with paper towels. When the potatoes are golden brown on both sides, remove them from the skillet and place them on the plate.

Place a cast-iron pan over medium heat and add the butter and melt. Add the sauerkraut and corned beef and press it down until it forms a single layer. Cook for 3 to 5 minutes, until golden brown on the bottom. Using a spatula, turn the mixture and continue cooking until the corned beef is brown on all sides. Fold in the potatoes.

Remove the pan from the heat and generously layer with the cheese. Place the pan under the broiler for about 2 minutes, or until the cheese is brown on top. Be careful here—it can burn quickly! Garnish with the dill and serve in the cast-iron pan with the rye bread.

AVOCADO TOAST WITH PICKLES, SPROUTS, AND RADISHES

Serves 2

Yes, of course, I wanted to put avocado toast in this book; it's one of my go-to morning meals. This one gives avocado the pickle treatment, adding both texture and flavor to this breakfast fave. It's as Instagrammable as it is satisfying, with NO filter needed.

1 medium avocado, halved and pitted, flesh removed

1 teaspoon pickle brine

Kosher salt and freshly ground black pepper

2 slices whole-grain bread, toasted

¼ cup thinly sliced pickles (such as dill)

¼ cup sprouts (such as alfalfa or radish)

2 radishes, thinly sliced

Extra-virgin olive oil

Red pepper flakes (optional)

In a small bowl, smash the avocado and brine with a fork or potato masher until smooth. Season with the salt and pepper.

Spread the avocado mixture evenly over the slices of bread. Top each with pickles, sprouts, and radishes.

Drizzle with a little olive oil and garnish with a sprinkle of red pepper flakes, if using. Serve immediately.

CHICKEN AND WAFFLE SANDO

Makes 4 to 6 waffles

These waffles fold sharp cheddar, chopped pickles, and smoky spices right into the batter. They're hearty enough to stand on their own or pair with fried chicken and a drizzle of hot sauce. These might not be your grandma's waffles, but they are yours now!

2⅔ cups all-purpose flour
4 teaspoons granulated sugar
2 teaspoons baking powder
1 teaspoon kosher salt
1 teaspoon black pepper
1 teaspoon garlic powder
1 teaspoon smoked paprika
1 teaspoon dried or roughly chopped fresh dill
4 large eggs, at room temperature
1¾ cups buttermilk
4 tablespoons unsalted butter, melted
¼ cup Spicy Dill pickle brine
1⅓ cups shredded sharp cheddar cheese, divided
1 cup finely chopped Spicy Dill pickle chips
Pickle-Brined Fried Chicken (page 111)
Jalapeño Pickle–Apple Slaw (page 74)
Maple syrup or hot sauce, for serving
Pickle chips, for serving

Preheat a waffle iron according to the manufacturer's instructions.

In a large bowl, whisk together the flour, sugar, baking powder, salt, pepper, garlic powder, smoked paprika, and dill.

In a separate medium bowl, whisk the eggs. Add the buttermilk, melted butter, and brine, whisking until well combined.

Pour the wet ingredients into the dry ingredients and stir until just combined. Fold in 1 cup of the cheddar cheese and the pickles.

Lightly grease the waffle iron with cooking spray. Pour the appropriate amount of batter into the waffle iron and sprinkle with some of the remaining cheddar cheese. Cook for 4 to 5 minutes, until golden brown and crisp, following the manufacturer's instructions.

Transfer the waffles to a wire rack and repeat with the remaining batter.

Top each with a piece of Pickle-Brined Fried Chicken and Jalapeño Pickle–Apple Slaw. Serve open faced or add another waffle on top to make a sandwich. Serve with maple syrup or hot sauce and more pickle chips on the side.

PICKLE-BRINED CRISPY BREAKFAST POTATOES

Serves 4 to 6

A good breakfast potato can really make my day. A bad one? Well, let's not talk about that. I love these ones because you boil these bad boys in pickle brine, then sear them, then watch as the edges get so crispy they snap. Perfect for catching runny egg yolks or for when you're feeling indulgent and eating straight from the pan.

1½ pounds Yukon Gold potatoes, peeled and cut into ½-inch cubes

1 cup dill pickle brine

1 tablespoon cornstarch

2 tablespoons salted butter

2 tablespoons vegetable oil

1 large yellow onion, medium diced

1 large bell pepper, seeded and medium diced

½ teaspoon garlic powder

¼ teaspoon black pepper

½ teaspoon smoked paprika

¼ cup coarsely chopped dill pickles

2 tablespoons chopped fresh dill (optional)

Place the potatoes in a large pot and add the brine. Add enough water to cover the potatoes by 1 inch. Bring to a boil over high heat, then decrease the heat and simmer for 5 to 7 minutes, until the potatoes are just fork tender but not falling apart. Drain well, transfer to a large bowl, and toss with the cornstarch.

In a large cast-iron skillet over medium-high heat, add the butter and oil. Once melted and hot, add the potatoes in an even layer and cook, undisturbed, for about 5 minutes, or until the bottoms are deeply golden and crisp.

Add the onion and continue cooking, stirring occasionally, for about 5 minutes, or until the onion is cooked through and the potatoes are crispy on all sides. Add the bell pepper, garlic powder, pepper, and smoked paprika, stir to coat, and cook for 1 minute.

Remove from the heat and stir in the pickles. Transfer the potatoes to a serving dish and top with fresh dill, if using. Serve immediately.

HONEY MUSTARD PICKLE CREAM CHEESE

Makes about 1 cup

Cream cheese meets diced pickles meets a splash of brine for a spread that's well rounded and perfect for smearing on bagels. It's also great on crackers—or, honestly, eaten with a spoon. This spread is quick to make and quicker to disappear.

8 ounces whipped cream cheese

¼ cup Honey Mustard pickle chips, finely chopped

1 to 2 tablespoons Honey Mustard pickle brine

In a medium bowl, combine the cream cheese and pickles. Stir in 1 tablespoon brine, mixing until smooth and evenly incorporated. Add more brine, a little at a time, until the cream cheese reaches your desired texture and tang.

Serve spread on bagels, toast, or crackers. Store in an airtight container in the refrigerator for up to 5 days.

PICKLE MILK BISCUITS

CHRIS ABOUABDO OF FOODBEAST

BACKSTORY WRITTEN BY CHRIS I almost never have buttermilk. You know what I almost always have? An empty jar of Kaylin + Kaylin pickles in the back of my fridge. The last pickle devoured weeks ago but delicious brine in abundance. I wouldn't dare pour it down the drain, but I don't quite have the courage to drink it neat. Maybe you can relate. Maybe not. Either way, here's a recipe to make when you've made so many of the other recipes in this book that you've got a stockpile of brine jars in the back of your fridge, like me.

If you look for buttermilk substitutes, people will tell you to add a tablespoon of lemon juice, or maybe a splash of vinegar, to a cup of milk. Nobody ever tells you to add pickle brine. I don't know why. The idea behind these substitutes is to add acid to milk to cause it to curdle a bit. Pickle brine has plenty of acid. So I pulled the thread of that metaphorical sweater until all that remained was a dream of pickle milk dancing around my mind. These biscuits were the best way I found to use it, but I encourage you to get creative and try anything that comes to your mind. Maybe pickle milk pancakes, or pickle milk fried chicken (that sounds good), or pickle milk pie, or pickle milk ranch (honestly, this might be even better than the biscuits), or . . . well, you get the point.

Biscuits

3½ cups all-purpose flour

1½ tablespoons baking powder

1 tablespoon granulated sugar

2 teaspoons kosher salt

1 cup (2 sticks) unsalted butter, cut into small cubes and frozen for 15 minutes

1 cup pickle milk (recipe follows), cold

Pickle brine, for brushing

Butter, pickles, and honey, for serving

Pickle Milk

⅓ cup pickle brine, such as Spicy Honey Mustard

⅔ cup whole milk

To make the pickle milk, in a small bowl or jar, stir together the brine and milk. Chill until ready to use.

Preheat the oven to 400°F. Line a baking sheet with parchment paper.

To make the biscuits, in a food processor, pulse together the flour, baking powder, sugar, salt, and butter until the butter is broken into small pea-sized pieces. Transfer the mixture to a large mixing bowl.

Add the pickle milk, stirring gently with a fork just until the dough begins to come together. It will be shaggy and crumbly—this is expected.

Turn the dough onto a clean surface and press it into a rough square. Cut into 4 equal pieces, stack them, and press down to form one cohesive square. Roll into a 1½-inch-thick slab. Repeat the cutting, stacking, and rolling process once more.

continued

Trim the edges with a sharp knife by cutting a very thin strip of dough from each side. (**Pro tip:** The sharper and cleaner you can make these cuts, the better rise you'll get from your biscuits. A sharp blade will glide through each individual layer with ease. A dull blade will smush the layers together and they'll stick shut, anchoring the top layers down and making it more difficult for them to rise and create the flaky texture we're after.) Then cut the dough into a 9 by 9-inch grid to yield 9 biscuits. Transfer the biscuits to the prepared baking sheet and freeze for 15 minutes.

Remove from the freezer and brush the tops with brine. Bake for 22 to 26 minutes, until golden brown.

Brush the biscuits with additional brine while still hot. Serve warm with butter, pickles, and honey—or use as the base for a breakfast sandwich. Store baked biscuits in an airtight container for up to 2 days or keep in the fridge for up to 5 days. Reheat in a 350°F oven for 8 to 10 minutes before serving for best texture.

MUNCHIES

A pickle is usually the snack. Straight from the jar, standing in front of the fridge with the door still open, maybe with a paper towel if you're being polite. But probably not, because you're at home and you're hungry and need a snack right now. Let the dog lick up the mess.

I took that snack and turned it into the foundation for even better ones. Pickles and brine aren't just on the side—they're in that luscious bite of Egg-Deviled Pickles (page 40), crispy Sauerkraut Korean Pancakes (page 35), Dill Pickle Focaccia (page 43), and a luxurious Galette (page 44) that gets attention—kind of like that guy on the sidewalk, pickle on a stick in hand, making everyone do a double take.

PICKLES IN A BLANKET (AKA REUBEN CROISSANTS)

Makes 8 rolls

Croissant dough wrapped around corned beef, Swiss, sauerkraut, and a cornichon makes for a portable Reuben. Yes, handheld treats that are excellent for brunch, an afternoon snack, a no-fuss party tray—or whenever you darn well want it.

All-purpose flour, for dusting
1 (8-count) can refrigerated crescent roll dough
8 teaspoons mustard, divided
8 deli slices corned beef, divided
8 deli slices Swiss cheese, divided
8 tablespoons mustard sauerkraut, divided
8 cornichons, divided
1 egg, beaten
Poppy seeds, for topping
Sesame seeds, for topping

Preheat the oven to 375°F. Line a baking sheet with parchment paper. Lightly flour a surface.

Unroll the crescent dough onto the prepared surface. Gently stretch each triangle to about twice its original length.

Working with one triangle at a time, spread 1 teaspoon mustard over the entire surface using an offset spatula. Layer one slice of the corned beef and one slice of the Swiss cheese over the dough.

Place 1 tablespoon sauerkraut in a small line near the wide end of the triangle. Set a cornichon on top of the sauerkraut, then roll the dough tightly and form into a crescent shape. Place on the prepared baking sheet.

Repeat with the remaining crescent rolls and remaining filling ingredients, spacing the finished rolls 2 inches apart on the baking sheet.

Brush the tops with the egg and sprinkle with the poppy and sesame seeds.

Bake for 10 to 12 minutes, until the rolls are golden brown. Serve warm.

SAUERKRAUT KOREAN PANCAKES

Makes 2 pancakes

Loaded with vegetables and sauerkraut, these savory pancakes fry to a lacy edge with a tender middle. The dipping sauce—salty, acidic, and lightly sweet—brings everything together. One taste and you'll keep finding excuses to make them.

Dipping Sauce

2 tablespoons soy sauce

1 tablespoon rice wine vinegar

2 teaspoons sesame oil

2 teaspoons maple syrup

1 garlic clove, peeled and minced

½ teaspoon sesame seeds

1 green onion, white and green parts, finely chopped

Pancake Batter

½ cup all-purpose flour

1 tablespoon cornstarch

½ teaspoon kosher salt

½ cup cold water

½ cup grated carrots

½ red or orange bell pepper, seeded and julienned

½ cup sriracha sauerkraut

1 tablespoon finely chopped garlic

2 green onions, white and green parts, finely chopped

Neutral oil (such as avocado oil), for frying

To make the dipping sauce, in a small bowl, whisk together all the ingredients until well combined. Set aside until ready to serve.

To make the pancake batter, in a medium bowl, whisk together the flour, cornstarch, salt, and water until smooth.

Fold in the carrots, bell pepper, sauerkraut, garlic, and green onions, mixing gently until the vegetables are evenly coated. The batter will be loose but should hold the veggies together.

Heat about ½ inch of oil in a large skillet or frying pan over medium heat until shimmering but not smoking.

Working in batches, scoop about ¼ cup batter into the pan for each pancake. Flatten gently with a spatula and cook for 4 to 5 minutes per side, until golden brown and crispy.

Transfer the pancakes to a wire rack or paper towel–lined plate to drain.

Cut the pancakes into 4 to 6 pieces and serve warm with the dipping sauce.

JALAPEÑO PICKLE AND CREAM CHEESE RANGOONS

Makes 20

I always used to think rangoons looked like a chore to make, but they couldn't be easier . . . and more delicious, thanks to the addition of Jalapeño pickles! You just tuck the creamy filling into wonton wrappers for a snack you'll be popping in your mouth like popcorn. They bake or air-fry into pockets that shatter in your mouth.

8 ounces cream cheese, at room temperature

4 green onions, finely chopped, white parts only

5 Jalapeño pickles, finely chopped

2 garlic cloves, peeled and finely minced

1 teaspoon sugar

1 tablespoon light soy sauce

20 wonton wrappers

1 egg, beaten

Fresh cilantro, for garnish

1 cup sweet Thai chili sauce, for serving

Preheat an air fryer to 350°F or the oven to 400°F.

In a medium bowl, mix together the cream cheese and the white parts of the green onion. Mix in the pickles, garlic, sugar, and soy sauce until well combined.

Place about ½ tablespoon filling in the center of each wonton wrapper. Lightly brush the edges with the egg. Pinch the corners together to form a diamond shape, keeping the bottom flat. Pinch the sides to seal the pouch completely, making sure there are no air pockets.

Spray the rangoons generously with cooking spray. To cook, place them in an air fryer for 5 to 7 minutes or bake them in an oven for 10 to 15 minutes, until golden brown and crisp.

Garnish with the cilantro and serve with the chili sauce for dipping.

BACON-WRAPPED PICKLES

Makes 12

I love using pickles as a vessel, and here I stuff them with cheddar and wrap them in smoky bacon. Each piece balances salt, fat, and crunch into one melty package. They tend to vanish as soon as they hit the table, so make sure you get some before serving.

6 whole dill pickles
12 cheddar cheese sticks
12 slices thick-cut bacon
Ranch dressing or any favorite dipping sauce, for serving

Preheat the oven to 350°F. Line a baking sheet with parchment paper.

Slice the pickles in half lengthwise. Using a small spoon, scoop out a shallow cavity from the center of each half to make room for the cheese. Discard the insides.

Place one cheese stick in the hollowed-out center of each pickle half.

Wrap one slice of bacon around each stuffed pickle half. Secure with a toothpick if needed.

Place on a baking sheet and bake for 10 to 15 minutes, until the bacon is browned and crisp.

Serve immediately with a side of ranch dressing.

EGG-DEVILED PICKLES

Makes 12

Think of this as the love child of deviled eggs and pickles. Instead of the classic egg-white halves, the seasoned yolk filling gets spooned into hollowed-out pickle "cups." It's a potluck contribution that makes people double-dip for more.

3 large dill pickles
4 hard-boiled egg yolks
2 teaspoons mayonnaise
1 teaspoon mustard
½ teaspoon paprika
Kosher salt and freshly ground black pepper
Fresh dill, for garnish

Cut the ends off each pickle, then slice each pickle into 4 equal pieces to make 12 pickle "cups." Using a small spoon, scoop out the centers of each piece to form a cavity, being careful not to scoop all the way through to the bottom.

In a medium bowl, combine the egg yolks, mayonnaise, mustard, paprika, salt, and pepper. Mix until smooth. Transfer the filling to a piping bag fitted with a star tip or to a resealable plastic bag with one corner snipped.

Pipe the egg mixture into the center of each pickle cup. Garnish with a small sprig of dill.

DILL PICKLE FOCACCIA

Makes 1 (9 by 13-inch) focaccia

Focaccia is one of the best breads around. And part of the fun is topping it however you like. This soft, airy, chewy Italian favorite gets scattered with chopped pickles, dill, and red pepper flakes before baking. When it comes out piping hot, you could serve it as a side, but honestly, you'll probably just tear off a piece to savor the pickles while they're still warm.

1¼ cups lukewarm water (90°F to 100°F)

1 cup plus 1 tablespoon pickle brine, at room temperature, divided

2¼ teaspoons (1 packet) instant yeast

4 cups (500 grams) all-purpose flour

1 teaspoon kosher salt

5 tablespoons extra-virgin olive oil, divided

½ cup chopped Spicy Dill pickle chips

1 teaspoon flaked salt (such as Maldon)

1 teaspoon dried dill

¼ teaspoon red pepper flakes

In a large mixing bowl, combine the water, 1 cup of the brine, and the yeast. Let sit for about 5 minutes, or until foamy.

Add the flour and salt and mix with a wooden spoon or spatula until a wet, sticky dough forms.

Knead the dough for about 5 minutes, or until smooth and elastic.

Add 2 tablespoons of the olive oil to the bowl and turn the dough to coat. Cover the bowl with plastic wrap, pressing it directly against the surface of the dough. Refrigerate overnight for 12 to 24 hours.

Preheat the oven to 425°F. Grease a 9 by 13-inch baking pan with 1 tablespoon of the olive oil.

Transfer the dough to the prepared pan and gently stretch it to fit. Let it rest at room temperature for 2 to 4 hours, until puffy and bubbly.

Drizzle the remaining 2 tablespoons olive oil over the surface. Scatter the pickles evenly across the top; drizzle with the remaining 1 tablespoon brine; and sprinkle with the salt, dill, and red pepper flakes. Using your fingers, gently dimple the dough, pressing slightly.

Bake for 30 to 40 minutes, until golden brown and crisp around the edges. Let cool slightly before serving.

FALAFEL WITH CHOPPED PICKLES

Makes about 25

Falafels are crispy spiced chickpea balls that are delicious on their own, but adding pickles to the mixture gives them a new dimension that's bright and lively. Pair with tzatziki, friends, and a pickle spear—because why not?

1½ cups dried chickpeas, soaked overnight, then drained
½ small yellow onion, peeled and roughly chopped
3 garlic cloves, peeled
1 bunch fresh flat-leaf parsley
1 bunch fresh dill
20 dill pickle chips
1 teaspoon ground cumin
1 teaspoon ground coriander
1 teaspoon baking powder
½ teaspoon cayenne pepper
1 teaspoon kosher salt
1 teaspoon black pepper
3 tablespoons all-purpose flour
Neutral oil (such as vegetable or canola oil), for frying
Tzatziki (page 61), for serving

In a food processor, working in batches, pulse the chickpeas, onion, garlic, parsley, dill, and pickle chips until finely chopped. Add the cumin, coriander, baking powder, cayenne, salt, pepper, and flour. Pulse until the mixture resembles coarse sand, scraping down the sides as needed. Do not purée.

Transfer the mixture to a medium bowl and stir to combine evenly. Scoop about 2 tablespoons of the mixture to form into balls or small patties. Line a baking sheet with parchment paper. Place the falafel on the prepared sheet and refrigerate for 30 minutes.

In a deep skillet or saucepan, heat 2 inches of oil to 350°F. Fry the falafel in batches, 2 to 3 minutes per side, turning occasionally, until golden brown and crispy. Drain on paper towels.

Serve warm with the tzatziki.

SAUERKRAUT LATKES

Makes 8 to 10

I grew up with latkes in their most traditional form: crispy on the outside, tender inside, and always served with sour cream and applesauce. So at first, the idea of straying from that classic felt almost sacrilegious. But then I tried this variation, and it just clicked. The familiar comfort of tradition is still there, but with a tangy, sour twist that brightens things up and makes the whole dish feel fresh and a little modern.

2 cups well-drained sauerkraut, roughly chopped

1 small yellow onion, roughly chopped

2 medium russet potatoes, peeled and roughly chopped

2 large eggs

¼ cup all-purpose flour or matzo meal

½ teaspoon baking powder

Kosher salt and freshly ground black pepper

Neutral oil (such as canola or vegetable oil), for frying

Herbs, for garnish

Sour cream or applesauce, for serving

In a food processor fitted with a grater attachment, grate the sauerkraut (to make it even smaller!), onion, and potatoes. Transfer the mixture to a salad spinner and spin briefly to release excess moisture.

Transfer the mixture to a large bowl and stir in the eggs, flour, baking powder, salt, and pepper. Place the mixture in a fine-mesh strainer set over a medium bowl to continue draining while you cook.

In a large heavy-bottomed skillet, heat ¼ inch of oil over medium-high heat until shimmering but not smoking.

Working in batches, scoop about ⅓ cup batter into the skillet for each latke, gently pressing with a spatula to flatten. Fry for 3 to 4 minutes per side, until golden and crisp, adjusting the heat as needed to avoid burning.

Transfer the cooked latkes to a paper towel–lined plate to drain. Repeat with the remaining batter.

Garnish and serve hot, with sour cream or applesauce.

DILL-PICKLED CASHEWS

Makes about 2 cups

Cashews are already good on their own, but I don't settle for good—I want extraordinary. So I bathe them in pickle liquid, vinegar, and spices, letting the flavors infuse before roasting them to a crisp, fragrant finish.

2 teaspoons dill weed
2 teaspoons milk powder
2 teaspoons kosher salt
1 teaspoon nutritional yeast
¼ teaspoon garlic powder
¼ teaspoon mustard powder
¼ teaspoon onion powder
1 tablespoon white vinegar
1 tablespoon pickle brine
2 cups unsalted roasted cashews

Preheat the oven to 375°F. Line a large baking sheet with parchment paper.

In a medium bowl, whisk together the dill weed, milk powder, salt, nutritional yeast, garlic powder, mustard powder, and onion powder until thoroughly combined. Add the vinegar and brine and stir until smooth.

Add the cashews and toss to coat evenly.

Spread the cashews in a single layer on the prepared baking sheet.

Bake for about 10 minutes, stirring every couple of minutes, until fragrant and lightly golden.

Remove from the oven and let cool completely, about 30 minutes.

Store completely cooled cashews in an airtight container at room temperature for up to 2 weeks.

PICKLE SUSHI

Serves 1 to 2

Who says sushi needs rice and nori? Put this in front of your favorite sushi lover and watch their face when it hits their mouth. This twist on traditional sushi swaps out the rice for a hollowed-out dill pickle! Stuffed with creamy tuna salad and topped with spicy jalapeños, nacho cheese drizzle, and crushed Flamin' Hot Cheetos, these rolls are bursting with fun. They may not be traditional, but they ARE fiery and impossible to resist.

1 large dill pickle
½ cup Big Chunky Tuna Salad (page 78)
¼ cup crushed Flamin' Hot Cheetos
Melted nacho cheese, for drizzling
Green onion, for garnish

Cut both ends off the pickle. Using a small spoon or a coring tool, carefully hollow out the center, leaving enough pickle around the edges to hold its shape.

Fill the hollowed pickle completely with the tuna salad, packing it tightly. Chill for 10 to 15 minutes to firm up, if desired.

Slice the stuffed pickle crosswise into ½-inch-thick rounds, creating "sushi" pieces.

Sprinkle generously with the Cheetos and then drizzle with the nacho cheese. Garnish with the green onion.

NOTE: Feel free to switch up the fillings and toppings however you like. It's your playground.

EXTRA CHEESY, SPICY SWEET-AND-SOUR NACHOS

Serves 6 to 8

Nachos are a choose-your-own-adventure kind of snack or meal. For these, bury tortilla chips under taco-seasoned beef, Jalapeño pickles (instead of pickled jalapeños), beans, and corn, all melted together with gooey cheese. The final dollops of pico and guacamole are the cherries on top. Of course, these are perfect for sharing (or perfect for not sharing) on game day or movie night or any excuse to gather around the table.

1 tablespoon neutral oil (such as vegetable or coconut oil)

1 pound ground beef or ground chicken, turkey, or plant-based protein

1 (1-ounce) package taco seasoning

Pickle brine, reserved

10 ounces tortilla chips, divided

4 cups shredded Mexican-blend cheese, divided

12 ounces Spicy Queso (page 63) or 1 (12-ounce) can queso dip, divided

1 cup cooked black beans, divided

1 cup cooked yellow corn, divided

1 cup Jalapeño pickles

1 cup pico de gallo

1 cup guacamole

Preheat the oven to 400°F. Line a large baking sheet with parchment paper and set aside.

In a large skillet over medium heat, add the oil and cook the ground beef according to the taco seasoning package directions, substituting brine for the water.

Arrange half of the tortilla chips on the prepared baking sheet. Top with half of the cooked beef, half of the shredded cheese, half of the queso dip, half of the beans, and half of the corn.

Repeat the layering with the remaining chips, beef, cheese, queso dip, beans, and corn. Finish with the Jalapeño pickles on top.

Bake for 4 to 6 minutes, until the cheese is melted.

Top with the pico de gallo and guacamole. Serve immediately.

CAT CORA'S DILL PICKLE HUMMUS

Makes about 2 cups

Trust Iron Chef Cat Cora to reimagine hummus in a way that feels both classic and a little rebellious. Chickpeas, dill pickles, tahini, and olive oil blend into a dip that's carrot-lickin' good. Garlic and cumin provide the backbone, while the pickle adds a twist. It's the kind of mashup Cat's known for—comforting yet bold, and guaranteed to keep you coming back for another scoop (or three).

2 (16-ounce) cans chickpeas, drained

½ cup chopped dill pickles, plus more for garnish

½ cup tahini

¼ cup extra-virgin olive oil, plus more for serving

¼ cup pickle brine

3 garlic cloves, peeled

1 teaspoon ground cumin

Kosher salt and freshly ground black pepper

Pinch of crushed red pepper flakes

1 tablespoon chopped fresh dill, for garnish

Pita bread triangles or chips and sliced vegetables, for serving

In a food processor, combine the chickpeas, pickles, tahini, olive oil, brine, and garlic. Add the cumin, salt, pepper, and red pepper flakes. Blend until smooth. Taste and adjust the seasoning if needed.

Transfer to a bowl. Drizzle with olive oil and top with chopped pickles and dill. Serve with pita chips and sliced vegetables.

SPINACH-ARTICHOKE DIP

Serves 8

Meet the dip that never lasts long at a party, with or without the pickle treatment. Spinach and artichokes give it some substance, but let's be real—it's all about that bubbling skillet of molten cheese. The Sweet Heat pickle chips and pepper jack sneak in a hint of spice that elevates this particular version of this crowd favorite. Grab bread, crackers, veggies, or a spoon and be prepared to guard your spot by the dish.

1 (16-ounce) package frozen spinach, thawed and thoroughly drained

1 (14-ounce) can quartered artichoke hearts, drained

20 Sweet Heat pickle chips, finely chopped

2 tablespoons extra-virgin olive oil

3 large garlic cloves, peeled and finely chopped

¼ teaspoon crushed red pepper flakes

Kosher salt and freshly ground black pepper

8 ounces cream cheese, cut into 1-inch pieces

1 cup shredded pepper jack cheese

½ cup sour cream

½ cup shredded Parmesan cheese

Baguette slices, for serving

Preheat the oven to broil.

In a food processor, pulse the spinach, artichokes, and pickles until coarsely chopped. Set aside.

In a medium cast-iron skillet over medium heat, heat the olive oil. Add the garlic and cook for about 30 seconds, stirring, until fragrant and softened. Add the spinach mixture and red pepper flakes. Season with salt and pepper. Cook for about 5 minutes, stirring frequently, or until most of the liquid has evaporated.

Decrease the heat to low. Add the cream cheese and pepper jack and stir with a wooden spoon for about 3 minutes, or until melted and fully incorporated. Stir in the sour cream and adjust the seasoning with additional salt and pepper if needed. Spread the mixture into an even layer and top with the Parmesan.

Broil on the top rack of the oven for about 5 to 10 minutes, until the top is golden and the dip is bubbling. Let rest briefly before serving. Serve warm with baguette slices.

CREAMY PICKLE RANCH DIP

Makes about 1 cup

Think of this as ranch dressing's pickle-obsessed cousin. Give it a little time to rest before serving—the flavors only get better once they've had a chance to mingle. Perfect with chips, veggies, pizza, or anything else you feel like dunking.

¾ cup sour cream
¼ cup buttermilk
1 tablespoon pickle brine
¼ cup finely chopped dill pickles
1 teaspoon chopped fresh dill
1 teaspoon chopped garlic
1 teaspoon chopped shallots
½ teaspoon kosher salt
¼ teaspoon black pepper
½ teaspoon paprika

In a medium bowl, whisk together the sour cream, buttermilk, and brine until smooth.

Stir in the pickles, dill, garlic, shallots, salt, pepper, and paprika until well combined. Cover and refrigerate for at least 30 minutes to allow the flavors to meld. Serve chilled. Store in a tightly sealed container in the fridge for up to 5 days; stir before serving.

BUFFALO CHICKEN DIP

Makes about 3 cups

All the best parts of buffalo wings—minus the sticky fingers—show up in this dip. The chicken turns tender and melty with Monterey Jack, while pickle brine and hot sauce bring just the right level of heat and bite. A scatter of green onions and extra pickles adds brightness; and the whole thing practically begs to be scooped up with celery, crackers, or honestly whatever you've got within reach.

4 ounces cream cheese, softened

½ cup sour cream

2 cups shredded cooked chicken

½ cup shredded Monterey Jack cheese

½ cup buffalo wing sauce, preferably Frank's RedHot

¼ cup finely chopped green onions, white and green parts

¼ cup chopped Jalapeño pickles

¼ cup Jalapeño pickle brine

Celery sticks and crackers, for serving

In a large bowl, beat the cream cheese with an electric mixer on medium speed for about 30 seconds, or until light and fluffy. Add the sour cream and beat for about 30 seconds more, or until smooth.

Add the chicken, cheese, buffalo sauce, green onions, pickles, and brine. Using a silicone spatula, mix until well combined.

Cover and refrigerate for at least 1 hour to allow the flavors to meld. Serve chilled with celery sticks and crackers. Store in a tightly sealed container in the fridge for up to 4 days.

TZATZIKI

Makes about 1½ cups

A staple of Greek tables for centuries, tzatziki is the cool, creamy sauce that shows up everywhere—from mezze spreads to platters of grilled meat. Traditionally made with yogurt, herbs, garlic, and cucumber, this version swaps in pickle brine for a little detour. Dill and mint keep it fresh, lemon zest adds brightness, and the result is a sauce that feels both classic and just a bit unexpected. Use it as a dip, dollop it on falafel, or spoon it over anything hot off the grill.

1 cup full-fat plain Greek yogurt
Juice of ½ lemon
¼ cup Classic Dill pickle brine
¼ cup extra-virgin olive oil
Finely grated zest of ½ lemon
½ cup finely chopped Classic Dill pickles
¼ cup finely chopped fresh dill
¼ cup finely chopped fresh mint
4 garlic cloves, peeled and minced
Kosher salt and freshly ground black pepper

In a medium bowl, whisk together the yogurt, lemon juice, and brine until smooth. Slowly whisk in the olive oil until incorporated.

Fold in the zest, pickles, dill, mint, and garlic. Season with salt and pepper to taste.

Cover and refrigerate until chilled. Serve cold with Falafel with Chopped Pickles (page 47).

Store in a tightly sealed container in the fridge for up to 3 to 4 days; stir before serving.

SPICY QUESO

Makes about 4 cups

This queso has attitude. Cheddar and pepper jack melt into a velvety pool that's studded with Jalapeño pickles, tomato, and a sprinkle of cilantro. Beer (mhmm) and evaporated milk keep it silky. I'm not one for strict rules, but the only real rule here is to eat it hot, preferably with a pile of chips and zero self-control. The second rule would be to double-dip, because we're all friends here.

2 tablespoons unsalted butter

½ medium yellow onion, finely chopped

1 jalapeño, seeded and finely chopped

3 garlic cloves, peeled and finely chopped

2 tablespoons all-purpose flour

½ cup Mexican lager

¼ teaspoon paprika

1 (12-ounce) can evaporated milk, divided

¼ cup chopped Jalapeño pickles

1 Roma tomato, finely chopped

¼ cup finely chopped fresh cilantro

2 teaspoons freshly squeezed lime juice

3 cups finely shredded sharp cheddar cheese

2 cups finely shredded pepper jack cheese

Kosher salt and freshly ground black pepper

Pickled jalapeños, for garnish

Tortilla chips, for serving

In a medium saucepan over medium heat, melt the butter. Add the onion, jalapeño, and garlic and sauté for 2 to 3 minutes, until softened. Stir in the flour and cook for about 1 minute, stirring constantly, until the mixture is golden and smells nutty.

Decrease the heat to low and slowly add the beer, stirring constantly with a wooden or plastic spatula. Stir in the paprika and evaporated milk. Bring to a gentle simmer and cook for 5 to 7 minutes, stirring frequently, until the mixture has reduced by half.

Stir in the pickles, tomato, cilantro, and lime juice. Remove from the heat and add the cheddar and pepper jack cheese. Stir until the cheese is melted and the queso is smooth. Season with salt and pepper to taste.

Transfer to a serving bowl. Garnish with the pickled jalapeños. Serve warm with tortilla chips.

Store in a tightly sealed container in the fridge for up to 3 days; reheat gently in a saucepan over low heat, stirring frequently, until warmed through and smooth.

CREAMY SWEET HEAT CORN

Makes about 4 cups

Creamed corn is one of those dishes that shows up whenever comfort is on the menu. It's a staple at holiday tables like Thanksgiving, makes a cozy addition to summer cookouts when corn is at its sweetest, and has long been a favorite side in my house. This slightly fiery twist takes the familiar classic to the next level.

¼ cup (½ stick) unsalted butter

1 poblano pepper, seeded and finely diced

4 garlic cloves, peeled and minced

½ cup whole milk

4 ounces cream cheese, cut into small cubes

1 (16-ounce) bag frozen corn

½ cup finely chopped Sweet Heat pickle chips

½ teaspoon cayenne pepper

¼ teaspoon ground nutmeg

In a medium saucepan over medium-high heat, melt the butter. Add the poblano and garlic and sauté for about 4 minutes, or until browned.

Stir in the milk and cream cheese. Cook, stirring frequently, until the cream cheese is melted and the mixture is smooth.

Add the corn, pickles, cayenne, and nutmeg. Decrease the heat to low and simmer for about 15 minutes, stirring occasionally, or until heated through and thickened slightly. Serve warm.

SALADS

This chapter is packed with salads of all types, like Lobster Salad (page 75) and High-Level Burger Salad (page 77), and flavor-boosters—the dressings that wake up a salad. I'm talking Greek Goddess Dressing (page 66) and Ultimate Pickle Caesar Dressing (page 67), and because I don't stop at the obvious, I threw in a Miso Vin (page 69).

GREEK GODDESS DRESSING

Makes about 3 cups

Herbs, avocado, Horseradish pickle brine, and lemon walk into a bowl . . . and out comes a thick, green, irresistible dressing. The avocado keeps things smooth and creamy, while dill and mint add multiple layers of serious complexity. Give it a night to chill and let the flavors cozy up—you'll thank yourself tomorrow.

3 garlic cloves, peeled

1 bunch fresh flat-leaf parsley, roughly chopped

1 bunch fresh dill, roughly chopped

¼ cup fresh mint leaves, roughly chopped

1 medium avocado, halved and pitted, flesh removed

½ cup Horseradish pickle brine

2 Horseradish pickles

½ cup extra-virgin olive oil

1 teaspoon red chili flakes

Juice of 1 lemon

In a blender, combine all the ingredients. Blend until smooth and creamy.

Transfer to a container with a tight-fitting lid. Cover and refrigerate for 12 to 24 hours to allow the flavors to develop fully. Store in a tightly sealed container in the fridge for up to 3 to 4 days; stir before serving and add a squeeze of lemon if the avocado begins to brown.

ULTIMATE PICKLE CAESAR DRESSING

Makes about 3 cups

Caesar dressing gets a twist with pickle chips and brine. Anchovies, garlic, and Parmesan keep it classic, while the brine adds a bright, lively note that works beautifully over kale, romaine, or any greens you love. I especially enjoy drizzling it over roasted vegetables or grilled chicken.

1 large egg yolk

4 anchovy fillets

6 garlic cloves, peeled and grated or minced

1 tablespoon Dijon mustard

1 tablespoon Worcestershire sauce

Juice of 1 lemon

½ cup plain Greek yogurt, full or 2% milkfat

10 Classic Dill pickle chips

⅓ cup finely grated Parmesan cheese

¼ teaspoon kosher salt

1 tablespoon black pepper

¾ cup extra-virgin olive oil

In a blender, combine the egg yolk, anchovies, garlic, mustard, Worcestershire sauce, lemon juice, yogurt, pickles, Parmesan, salt, and pepper. Blend until smooth.

With the blender running, slowly drizzle in the olive oil until fully emulsified.

Transfer to an airtight container and refrigerate for at least 2 hours before serving. The dressing can be stored in the refrigerator for up to 1 week.

SPICY ITALIAN-ISH DRESSING

Makes about 1½ cups

This vinaigrette brings together olive oil, vinegar, Dijon, and pickle brine, accented with oregano and basil. I love how a dusting of nutritional yeast adds a flavor you can't quite put your finger on, while a touch of red pepper flakes delivers just enough heat to make you perk up a little.

½ cup extra-virgin olive oil
½ cup red wine vinegar
¼ cup Horseradish pickle brine
1 tablespoon Dijon mustard
1 tablespoon honey
½ teaspoon garlic powder
1 teaspoon dried oregano
½ teaspoon dried basil
½ teaspoon onion powder
1 tablespoon nutritional yeast
¼ teaspoon crushed red pepper flakes

In a medium bowl, whisk together all the ingredients until well combined. Store in a tightly sealed container in the fridge for up to 2 weeks; shake or whisk before serving.

MISO VIN

Makes about 1 cup

Miso paste is a rich, salty, and deeply savory fermented soybean paste that gives this dressing its earthy foundation. A splash of pickle brine lifts the flavors, while a hint of maple syrup adds gentle sweetness. Toasted sesame oil weaves everything together with a warm, nutty aroma. It's great with crisp greens or roasted vegetables!

2 garlic cloves, peeled and minced
1 shallot, minced
2 tablespoons soy sauce
¼ cup Sweet Heat pickle brine
2 tablespoons light miso paste
1 tablespoon maple syrup
1 tablespoon plain Greek yogurt, full or 2% milkfat
½ cup vegetable oil
1 tablespoon sesame oil

In a medium bowl, whisk together all the ingredients until smooth and fully combined. Store in a tightly sealed container in the fridge for up to 5 days; whisk before serving.

Left to right: My Daughter's Favorite Sauce (pg. 72), Greek Goddess Dressing (pg. 66), Spicy Italian-ish Dressing (pg. 68), Ultimate Pickle Caesar Dressing (pg. 67)

MY DAUGHTER'S FAVORITE SAUCE

JESSI KAYLIN

Makes 1 cup

My daughter, whom I adoringly refer to as "Face," has made this so many times that she could make it with her eyes closed. Actually, you can too—it's that easy. Ketchup, Dijon, finely chopped pickles, and a splash of brine are mixed together in a sauce that goes with the High-Level Burger Salad (page 77), or anytime, anywhere.

4 tablespoons ketchup

1 tablespoon Dijon mustard

1 Kosher Dill pickle, finely chopped

10 Honey Mustard pickle chips, finely chopped

3 tablespoons Honey Mustard pickle brine, divided

In a small bowl, stir together the ketchup and Dijon mustard. Add the dill pickle and Honey Mustard pickle chips. Slowly whisk in the brine, 1 tablespoon at a time, until the dressing reaches your preferred texture. Use immediately or refrigerate for up to 5 days.

WARM HONEY MUSTARD SMASHED POTATO SALAD

Makes about 6 cups

Most potato salads sit cold in a bowl, dressed in mayo and maybe overlooked as "another potato salad." But truthfully, adding pickle brine brightens it up tremendously and gives it new life. Like a regular potato salad, you want to lightly smash the spuds so each bite holds on to warm, bacon-studded honey mustard dressing with a surprising splash of pickle brine.

2½ pounds baby red potatoes
12 ounces thick-cut bacon, diced
1 medium yellow onion, finely diced
3 garlic cloves, peeled and minced
2 tablespoons whole-grain mustard
½ cup Honey Mustard pickle brine
¼ cup honey
½ cup finely chopped Honey Mustard pickle chips
1 tablespoon chopped fresh dill
1 tablespoon chopped curly parsley
1½ tablespoons freshly squeezed lemon juice
Kosher salt and freshly ground black pepper

Bring a large pot of salted water to a boil and line a baking sheet with parchment. Add the potatoes to the pot and cook for 10 to 15 minutes, until fork tender. Drain and transfer to the baking sheet. Using a heavy-bottomed glass bowl, gently press each potato until smashed. Set aside.

In a medium skillet over medium-high heat, cook the bacon until crisp. Using a slotted spoon, transfer the bacon to a plate, leaving the rendered fat in the pan.

Return the pan to medium heat. Add the onion and garlic and cook for about 4 minutes, stirring, until soft and translucent. Stir in the mustard, brine, and honey. Bring to a boil, then decrease the heat to low and simmer for about 5 minutes, or until the mixture is reduced by half.

Add the smashed potatoes to the skillet and gently toss to coat in the warm dressing. Fold in the bacon, pickles, dill, and parsley. Add the lemon juice and season with salt and pepper to taste. Serve warm.

Store in an airtight container in the fridge for up to 3 days.

JALAPEÑO PICKLE–APPLE SLAW

Serves 4

I love slaw. I love it on everything. I love it by itself. I love it on tacos. And I love it even more with matchstick-cut pickles tossed with cabbage, carrots, apples, and a creamy mustard-brine dressing. The apple's gentle sweetness plays well against the heat of the Jalapeño pickles. A perfect counterpoint to your favorite slaw counterpart.

- **¼ cup Jalapeño pickle brine**
- **¼ cup sour cream**
- **1 tablespoon whole-grain Dijon mustard**
- **½ teaspoon celery seed**
- **½ teaspoon kosher salt**
- **½ teaspoon black pepper**
- **4 cups shredded purple cabbage**
- **½ cup shredded carrots**
- **½ cup Jalapeño pickles, cut into matchsticks**
- **¼ cup thinly sliced red onion**
- **1 medium Fuji apple, cut into matchsticks**

In a large bowl, whisk together the brine, sour cream, mustard, celery seed, salt, and pepper until smooth.

Add the cabbage, carrots, pickles, red onion, and apple. Toss well to coat.

Cover and refrigerate for at least 30 minutes to allow the flavors to meld. Serve chilled.

Store in a tightly sealed container in the fridge for up to 2 days; toss before serving.

LOBSTER SALAD

Serves 2 to 3

Sweet, succulent lobster gets tossed with a creamy dressing and a little crunch from crisp veggies, making each bite indulgent without being heavy. Serve it chilled in a pickle boat for a fancy-ish lunch that redefines a lobster roll.

1½ cups cooked lobster meat (tails and claws), chopped

¼ cup mayonnaise

1 celery stalk, finely diced

1 tablespoon finely diced red onion

2 tablespoons diced yellow bell pepper or cucumber

1 teaspoon freshly squeezed lemon juice

Kosher salt and freshly ground black pepper

Pinch of cayenne pepper (optional)

In a medium bowl, combine the lobster, mayonnaise, and celery. Stir in the onion and bell pepper. Add the lemon juice, then season with salt and pepper to taste, and the cayenne, if using. Mix gently until evenly coated. Chill for 10 to 15 minutes, if desired, or serve immediately.

HIGH-LEVEL BURGER SALAD

Serves 4 to 6

Think of this as a burger without the bun, built to eat with a fork instead of your hands. Around my family, we call it "high level" because everything gets chopped up, piled sky high, and served like the over-the-top salad it is.

Meat

16 ounces 92/8 ground beef or turkey

¼ cup freshly grated Wisconsin cheddar cheese

¼ cup freshly grated Colby Jack cheese

Salad

2 heads romaine lettuce, chopped

2 Roma tomatoes, chopped

1 medium avocado, halved and pitted, flesh removed, chopped

¼ cup chopped red onion

Shredded cheddar cheese

Chopped pickles (any variety)

1 Jalapeño pickle, chopped

1 Kosher Dill pickle, chopped

Sesame seeds, for garnish

My Daughter's Favorite Sauce (page 72)

To make the meat, in a skillet over medium heat, cook the ground beef until browned and cooked through, breaking it into small pieces as it cooks. Remove from the heat and stir in the cheeses until melted and evenly distributed. Set aside to cool slightly.

To make the salad, in a large bowl, combine the romaine, tomatoes, avocado, red onion, cheese, chopped pickles, Jalapeño pickle, and Kosher Dill pickle. Top with the warm cooked meat mixture and a sprinkle of sesame seeds.

Drizzle My Daughter's Favorite Sauce (page 72) over the salad and serve immediately.

BIG CHUNKY TUNA SALAD

Makes about 2 cups

This tuna salad is an easy-to-whip-up lunch or dinner tucked between two slices of your favorite sandwich bread or scooped atop a bed of lettuce or shoved into hollowed-out pickles. The trick here is using hummus in the mix, which gives this recipe such a fun flavor among the crunchy pickles. Make sure to mix it gently to maintain the big chunks of tuna!

2 (5-ounce) cans tuna, packed in water, drained

3 green onions, white and green parts, finely chopped

1 Jalapeño pickle, finely chopped

1 Classic Dill pickle, finely chopped

1 clove garlic, peeled and finely chopped

¼ cup chopped red onion

4 tablespoons plain hummus

1 teaspoon everything bagel seasoning

Pinch of kosher salt and freshly ground black pepper

In a medium bowl, combine the tuna, green onions, Jalapeño pickle, Classic Dill pickle, garlic, red onion, and hummus. Mix until well combined. Season with the everything bagel seasoning, salt, and pepper to taste. Chill in the fridge for at least 30 minutes before serving.

Serve over leafy greens, spoon into a sandwich, or enjoy as is.

TOPPED

Maybe putting pickles *next to* the meal or *into* the meal might not be enough when sometimes you want them to *be* the meal.

Here you'll turn whole pickles into little boats and load them up with toppings like tuna salad, lox and cream cheese, and Hot Cheetos. Some combos are classic. Some are straight-up unhinged. All of them are ridiculously fun.

This section is where we go all in. Dills become vessels. Chips become nachos. It's messy. And it's one of the most joyful ways I've seen people interact with pickles—building bites, mixing textures, and asking, "Wait . . . am I really eating this?"

Yes. Yes, you are.

PICKLE BOATS AND MINI BOATS

Pickle boats are more than just a snack—they're tiny edible vessels just waiting to be loaded with whatever deliciousness you can dream up. Crispy, briny, and perfectly shaped to cradle fillings, they make every bite a little adventure. From creamy cheeses and bacon to, yes, Nutella, the possibilities are endless, and each boat is an invitation to get creative (and a little messy). Perfect for parties or just a solo snack attack, pickle boats turn ordinary ingredients into handheld dreams.

HOW TO MAKE A PICKLE BOAT:

Whole pickle (extra large for full-size boats, regular for minis)

Cut the pickles in half lengthwise. For full-size boats, half of a large pickle serves one; for mini boats, three halves of a small pickle make a serving. Using a spoon or small utensil, gently scoop out the seeds and soft interior to create a hollow "boat," being careful not to damage the skin. Pat the inside and outside dry with a paper towel before filling.

Spoon in your favorite ingredients, layering flavors and textures as desired, and serve immediately.

Pickle Boats

1 pickle boat

¼ cup crunchy topping (such as Cheese Cheetos, Doritos, Hot Cheetos, Fritos, Takis, Ruffles, or any bagged chips you want!)

1 tablespoon melted nacho cheese

Put the crunchy topping in a resealable plastic bag, or if it is a single-serving bag, open the top of the bag. Use your hands or any utensil to crush the topping into a crunchy crumble with some fine dust. Fill half of the pickle with the crushed topping. Then, drizzle the nacho cheese across the topping. Serve immediately.

Cream Cheese Boats

Everything Cream Cheese Boat

1 pickle boat

2½ tablespoons cream cheese

½–1 teaspoon bagel seasoning

Lox and Everything Cream Cheese Boat

1 pickle boat

2½ tablespoons cream cheese

1 ounce lox

½–1 teaspoon everything bagel seasoning

Lox and Caper Cream Cheese Boat

1 pickle boat

2½ tablespoons cream cheese

1 ounce lox

1 teaspoon capers

Bacon Bits Cream Cheese Boat

1 pickle boat

2½ tablespoons cream cheese

1½ tablespoons bacon bits

Spread the cream cheese evenly along the bottom of the pickle boat, creating a smooth base for your toppings. Choose your flavor additions (everything seasoning, lox, capers, bacon bits, or anything savory you like) and sprinkle or layer them over the cream cheese. Press them lightly so they stick into the surface without sinking. The cream cheese should act as the anchor, while the toppings stay visible on top for texture and flavor. Serve immediately.

1
2
3
4
5
6
7
8

1. Classic Dill Pickle Chips + Cheetos + Nacho Cheese; **2.** Pickle Boat + Peanut Butter + Nutella + Pretzels; **3.** Pickle Boat + Cream Cheese + Bacon Bits; **4.** Pickle Boat + Tuna Salad + Everything Bagel Seasoning; **5.** Pickle Boat + Fritos + Nacho Cheese; **6.** Pickle Boat + Lobster Salad + Chives; **7.** Pickle Boat + Cream Cheese + Lox + Capers; **8.** Sweet Heat Pickle Chips + Maple Syrup; **9.** Pickle Boat + Takis + Nacho Cheese; **10.** Pickle Sandwich with turkey, cheddar, Flamin' Hot Cheetos; **11.** Pickle Boat + Tuna Salad in a Lettuce Wrap + Classic Dill Pickle Chips; **12.** Pickle Boat + Cream Cheese + Lox + Everything Bagel Seasoning; **13.** Pickle Boat + Pastrami + Mustard + Sauerkraut + Swiss; **14.** Classic Dill Pickle Chips + Flamin' Hot Cheetos + Nacho Cheese (Recipes on pages 80–81, 84–86)

Peanut Butter and Nutella Boats

1 pickle boat

2 tablespoons peanut butter

1 tablespoon Nutella

1 tablespoon pretzels or other salty snack (optional)

Spread the peanut butter evenly along the bottom of the pickle boat, creating a thick base. Add a drizzle or layer of Nutella on top of the peanut butter, letting it swirl naturally. For extra crunch, sprinkle pretzel pieces over the Nutella and press them lightly so they stay in place. The peanut butter anchors the fillings, while the Nutella and pretzels add sweetness and texture on top. Serve immediately for the best balance of salty-sweet flavors.

Salad in a Boat

1 pickle boat

3 tablespoons tuna or chicken salad

½–1 teaspoon everything bagel seasoning or bacon bits (or go crazy and top with any favorite crunchy topping)

1½ tablespoons potato chips

Spoon the salad into the hollow of the pickle boat, filling it generously so it reaches the top edge. Sprinkle a light layer of seasoning across the salad for added flavor. For crunch, top with the crushed chips, pressing them gently into the surface so they stick. The salad provides the hearty filling, while the chips add the finishing texture on top. Serve immediately.

PICKLE SANDWICHES AND SLIDERS

What really makes a sandwich a sandwich? Is it the bread, the fillings, or just the joy of stacking flavors? With these pickle-powered sammies, I toss the bread aside and let juicy pickles hold the cheese, meat, and crunchy toppings. It's all the satisfaction of a sandwich—just a little crazier.

Deli Sandwich

1 large pickle

2 slices of your favorite deli meat (such as ham, turkey, roast beef, etc.)

2 slices cheese

Crunchy topping (such as potato chips, Takis, Fritos, bacon bits, fried onions, or shredded lettuce)

Nacho cheese or condiment of choice (optional)

Slice a large pickle in half lengthwise and gently scoop out the centers from both halves. On one pickle half, layer a slice of meat, both slices of cheese, your chosen crunchy topping, and a second slice of meat. Place the other pickle half on top to form a sandwich and secure with a large toothpick on each side. Cut in half to serve. For sliders, secure with three toothpicks across the sandwich and cut into thirds for bite-size, party-ready portions. Serve immediately.

Open-Face Pickle Reuben

1 large pickle

2 tablespoons sauerkraut

Mustard

3 slices pastrami or corned beef

1 slice Swiss cheese

Slice a large pickle in half lengthwise and scoop out just one half to form a boat. Fill the boat with sauerkraut, tossing with mustard beforehand if desired for extra flavor. Line a plate with parchment. On the plate, layer the meat and Swiss cheese and microwave for about 30 seconds, or until the cheese is melted. Transfer the hot meat and cheese mixture into the pickle boat and serve immediately.

PICKLE CHIPS

Pickle waffle chips usually go it alone—crunchy, salty, and perfectly content on their own. But I like to shake things up . . . literally. Tossed with crumbled toppings and drenched in hot nacho cheese, each chip becomes a little powerhouse of flavor. It's my way of turning the simple pickle chip into something unforgettable.

Nacho Chips

12–15 pickle waffle chips (¼ inch thick)

¼ cup crumbled crunchy topping (chips, fried onions, or bacon bits)

3 tablespoons melted nacho cheese

⅓ cup chili (optional)

Pat the pickle chips dry with a paper towel, then toss them in a mixing bowl with your chosen crumbled topping. Transfer the mixture to a small serving bowl and drizzle generously with the nacho cheese. Serve immediately.

Maple-y Chips

12–15 Sweet Heat pickle chips

3 tablespoons maple syrup

Pat the pickle chips dry with a paper towel, then toss them in a mixing bowl with the maple syrup. Transfer the mixture to a small serving bowl and serve immediately.

ENTREES

These recipes prove that pickles can be the star of the show—or at least the flavor that transforms a dish from a C-list celebrity to an Academy Award winner.

There's Pickle-Brined Fried Chicken (page 111) and Pickled Marinated Shrimp Ceviche (page 96) and even Neapolitan-style Mortadella and Pickle Pizza with Spicy Ranch (page 106) so good you'll skip going to pizzerias from here on out.

This is where you'll really stretch your muscles—chopping, brining, marinating, and getting playful with bold techniques that turn everyday meals into pickle-powered main events. Whether you're roasting, frying, smoking, stuffing, or just building the perfect Mile-High Melt (page 91), these recipes let pickles do more than sit on the side—they bring the whole thing together.

HONEY MUSTARD SALMON WITH PICKLEY RICE

Serves 4

This is such a turnkey way to make salmon delicious, and I'm making this twice, maybe three times a month. When dipping filets into a bath of Honey Mustard pickle brine and letting them marinate, it creates not only a robust flavor but also a soft texture when baked. Pair with pickle-infused rice for a well-rounded meal!

Salmon

4 (4-ounce) salmon fillets

1 cup Honey Mustard pickle brine

Pickley Rice

1½ cups cooked jasmine rice

¼ cup frozen peas

1½ ounces Honey Mustard pickle brine

Honey Mustard pickle chips, finely chopped (about 2 to 3 tablespoons)

Lemons, for serving

To make the salmon, place the salmon fillets in a resealable plastic bag. Add the brine, seal the bag, and turn to coat the fish. Refrigerate for 12 to 24 hours, turning the bag twice during marinating.

Preheat the oven to 400°F. Line a baking sheet with aluminum foil and lightly grease with cooking spray or olive oil.

Remove the salmon from the brine and place it on the prepared baking sheet. Discard the brine. Loosely cover with foil and bake for about 20 minutes, or until the salmon is opaque and flakes easily with a fork.

While the salmon bakes, prepare the rice. Place the peas in a fine-mesh strainer and rinse under hot water to thaw. Add the peas to the cooked rice along with the pickles and brine. Stir until well combined.

Serve the salmon over the top of Pickley Rice with lemon.

MILE-HIGH MELT

Serves 1

Do you like a Cuban sandwich, or do you love a Cuban sandwich? I love it. It's one of those sandwiches that will test your jaw! Roasted pork, ham, Swiss cheese, and pickles are layered between buttery toasted bread until it's stacked as tall as a skyscraper.

2 slices sourdough or white baguette, sliced lengthwise
½ tablespoon Honey Mustard pickle brine
2 teaspoons deli or Dijon mustard
5 ounces thick sliced roasted pork
5 ounces thinly sliced baked ham
2 slices Swiss cheese
8–10 Honey Mustard pickle chips
Unsalted butter, for cooking
Pickle spear, for serving

Drizzle the brine on one side of each piece of bread, and spread the mustard on one of those brine-drizzled pieces of bread. Layer the pork, ham, cheese, and pickles.

Place the top slice of bread on the sandwich and lightly brush both sides with butter. Grill for about 2 minutes on each side, either on a panini press or in a skillet, until browned. Cut in half and serve immediately with a pickle spear on top.

LADY AND LARDER'S YES, HONEY! SANDWICH

Serves 1

Created by the team at Lady and Larder, a beloved sister-owned shop, the Yes, Honey! Sandwich celebrates the craft and care that made their cheese and charcuterie business a community favorite. This well-composed turkey and ham sandwich is comforting in every bite, with shredded cheddar woven throughout so each mouthful has a creamy, melty touch that perfectly complements the tangy pickles and crisp vegetables.

2 slices sourdough or boule bread

½ tablespoon mayonnaise

3 ounces shaved roast turkey

3 ounces shaved smoked ham

2 ounces shredded cheddar cheese

2 ounces Honey Mustard pickle chips, chopped

1 ounce shaved red onion

Handful of shredded iceberg, romaine, or radicchio lettuce

Flaked salt (such as Maldon)

Extra-virgin olive oil and red wine vinegar, for drizzling

Spread the mayonnaise on one side of each slice of bread. Layer the turkey, ham, cheese, pickles, red onion, and lettuce on one slice. Sprinkle with salt and drizzle lightly with olive oil and vinegar. Close the sandwich with the other slice of bread and serve.

ULTIMATE PICKLE BACON BURGER

Serves 4

The secret to this burger is right in the patty. Finely chopped dill pickles get mixed straight into the ground beef, adding little bursts of moisture that keep the burgers juicy and deeply seasoned from the inside out. Stack them with cheddar, bacon, crisp veggies, and a swipe of special sauce and you've got a burger that balances richness with a sharp, satisfying bite in every mouthful. This recipe can easily be adapted to make smaller sliders if you prefer. This sauce is also great for dipping fries!

Sauce

¼ cup ketchup

¼ cup mayonnaise

1 tablespoon relish

1 tablespoon brown sugar

1 tablespoon pickle brine

Patties

1 pound 80/20 ground beef

¼ cup finely chopped Classic Dill pickles or Honey Mustard pickle chips

1 tablespoon black pepper

4 slices cheddar cheese

1 medium red onion, sliced into 4 rounds

Assembly

4 brioche buns, halved

4 leaves butter lettuce

4 slices tomato

4 slices cooked bacon

10 pickle slices

To make the sauce, in a food processor or blender, purée all the ingredients until smooth. Set aside.

To make the patties, in a medium bowl, combine the ground beef, pickles, and pepper. Form into 4 equal-size patties.

Heat a cast-iron skillet over medium-high heat. Cook the patties to your desired doneness, 3 to 4 minutes per side. Transfer to a resting rack and top each patty with a slice of cheese.

Add the onion rounds to the same skillet and cook for 3 to 4 minutes, flipping halfway through, until translucent.

To assemble, spread the sauce on the cut sides of each bun. Lightly toast the buns in the skillet, cut sides down, about 1 to 2 minutes, until golden. Remove from the pan and layer each bun with a lettuce leaf, tomato slice, onion, cheese-topped patty, bacon slice, and a few pickle slices. Top with the remaining bun half and serve.

PICKLED MARINATED SHRIMP CEVICHE

Serves 4 to 6

This ceviche gets its punch from a pickle-lime brine that "cooks" the shrimp—meaning that the acid in the brine changes the shrimp's texture and color, just like heat would, without any actual cooking. Using a glass bowl is key here: it keeps the brine from reacting with a metal bowl, so the shrimp stays fresh and perfectly opaque. Toss in red onion, cucumber, avocado, Jalapeño pickles, cilantro, and cherry tomatoes and you've got a refreshing dish that's perfect with tortilla chips, plantain slices, or even pickle chips.

Brine

½ cup dill pickle brine

½ cup freshly squeezed lime juice

3 tablespoons freshly squeezed lemon juice

1 pound raw shrimp, peeled, deveined, and chopped into bite-size pieces

Ceviche

½ teaspoon crushed red pepper flakes (optional)

1 garlic clove, peeled and smashed

½ cup finely diced red onion

½ cup diced cucumber

¼ cup finely chopped Jalapeño pickles

½ medium avocado, pitted, flesh removed, diced

¼ cup chopped fresh cilantro

½ cup cherry tomatoes, halved lengthwise

Kosher salt and freshly ground black pepper

Tortilla chips, plantain chips, or pickle chips, and limes, for serving

To make the brine, in a medium glass bowl, combine the pickle brine, lime juice, lemon juice, and shrimp. Cover and refrigerate for 2 to 4 hours, stirring once or twice, until the shrimp is opaque and fully "cooked" through. Drain and discard the brine.

Transfer the shrimp to a clean bowl. Add the red pepper flakes, if using, garlic, red onion, cucumber, pickles, avocado, cilantro, and tomatoes. Stir gently to combine. Season with salt and pepper to taste. Refrigerate for 10 to 15 minutes to allow the flavors to meld.

Serve chilled with tortilla chips, plantain chips, or pickle chips, and lime.

SESAME-PEANUT NOODLES WITH SMASHED HALF SOURS

Serves 2

These noodles are creamy and succulent. A sesame-peanut sauce gets a boost from pickle juice, while chopped half-sour pickles add bursts of crunch that make each bite more interesting. The hot noodles are swirled vigorously with the sauce using chopsticks or tongs, coating every strand in rich flavor. Topped with green onions, cilantro, and peanuts—and a little chili crisp if you like heat—this is a quick meal that feels anything but ordinary.

Noodles and Assembly

2 (8-ounce) packages udon noodles; or 4 ounces dried spaghetti, ramen, or soba noodles

¼ cup chopped half-sour pickles

1 green onion, white and green parts, thinly sliced

2 tablespoons chopped fresh cilantro

2 tablespoons chopped peanuts

Chili crisp, for serving (optional)

Sauce

3 tablespoons smooth peanut butter

1 tablespoon toasted sesame oil

1 tablespoon soy sauce

2 tablespoons pickle brine

1 tablespoon honey

1 tablespoon chili crisp

2 small garlic cloves, peeled and grated

To make the noodles, cook according to the package instructions. Reserve 2 tablespoons cooking water and drain the noodles.

To make the sauce, in a medium bowl, whisk together all the ingredients plus the reserved cooking water until smooth.

Add the hot noodles to the bowl and swirl vigorously using chopsticks or tongs until evenly coated with the sauce.

Divide the noodles between two bowls and top with the pickles, green onion, cilantro, peanuts, and additional chili crisp, if using. Serve immediately.

CHEESEBURGER-STUFFED POTATOES

JOY BAUER, MS, RD, CDN

Serves 4

A nationally recognized nutritionist and health expert, Joy Bauer is incredible at making comfort food both hearty and delicious. Take these baked potatoes, for instance. Melty cheese, savory turkey, and a bright pop of pickle turn a simple baked potato into a crave-worthy dish that's fun to eat and satisfying to the last bite. Any type of large potato will work. In the special sauce, mayonnaise gives a creamy flavor, or Greek yogurt adds a tangy twist.

Potatoes

4 large sweet potatoes or white potatoes

Extra-virgin olive oil

1 pound ground turkey (90 to 94% lean)

1 tablespoon soy sauce

1 tablespoon Worcestershire sauce

1 teaspoon garlic powder

1 teaspoon onion powder

½ teaspoon kosher salt, plus more for potatoes

¼ teaspoon black pepper

2 cups shredded cheddar cheese, divided

Special Sauce

¼ cup ketchup

¼ cup light mayonnaise or plain, low-fat Greek yogurt (2% milkfat)

Toppings

Pickle chips

Diced onions (optional)

Chopped tomatoes (optional)

Avocado slices (optional)

Minced fresh herbs (such as flat-leaf parsley or chives) (optional)

Crumbled turkey bacon (optional)

continued

To make the chicken, place the chicken breasts between two large sheets of parchment paper or wax paper. Using a meat tenderizer or rolling pin, pound the chicken until no more than ½ inch thick all around. Cut each breast in half to create 4 pieces. Place the chicken in a resealable plastic bag or bowl with the brine. Refrigerate for at least 30 minutes or up to overnight.

Preheat the oven to 450°F. Mist a baking sheet with nonstick spray or line with aluminum foil. If using a wire rack, place it on top of the baking sheet.

In a shallow bowl, whisk together the egg and mayonnaise. In a second shallow bowl, combine the breadcrumbs, garlic powder, onion powder, paprika, salt, and pepper. Working one at a time, lift each piece of chicken from the marinade, letting the excess drip off. Dip into the egg mixture, then coat with the breadcrumb mixture, pressing to adhere. Place the chicken on the prepared baking sheet or wire rack. Mist the tops with nonstick spray and sprinkle lightly with salt. Bake for about 20 minutes, or until the chicken reaches an internal temperature of 165°F and the tops are golden and crispy.

While the chicken is baking, make the sauce. In a small bowl, whisk together all the ingredients (including the honey, if using). Refrigerate until ready to serve.

To assemble, layer the bottom half of each bun with lettuce and tomato. Top with a chicken cutlet, a generous spoonful of sauce, and pickles. Cover with the top bun and serve immediately.

MORTADELLA AND PICKLE PIZZA WITH SPICY RANCH

DANIELE UDITI FROM PIZZANA

Makes 1 (12-inch) pizza

Chef Daniele Uditi, the LA-based master pizzaiolo and chef at Pizzana, is exactly that: a master. His pizza is so authentically perfect that it's hard not to take a bite and feel like you're sitting in a Neapolitan plaza. Inspired by Anthony Bourdain's favorite sandwich—fried mortadella with provolone, Dijon mustard, and mayonnaise on a toasted roll—this layers creamy cheeses, mortadella, and a hint of sweet-tart pickle, finished with a drizzle of spicy Calabrian ranch. And don't worry, Uditi's pizza dough recipe is included! Buon appetito!

Pizza Crust

1 (250-gram) 70 Percent Hydration Pizza Dough ball (page 107)

Toppings

60 grams provolone cheese, thinly sliced or shredded

80 grams fior di latte (a fresh cow's milk mozzarella), torn into chunks

2 to 3 tablespoons finely diced Honey Mustard pickle chips

8 to 10 thin slices mortadella

Extra-virgin olive oil

Freshly ground black pepper

Calabrian Ranch

3 tablespoons ranch dressing

1 teaspoon hot sauce (such as Frank's, Cholula, or sriracha)

¼ teaspoon smoked paprika

Pinch of cayenne pepper (optional)

Fresh basil or chopped herbs, for garnish

Place a pizza stone or steel in the oven and preheat to 500°F to 550°F. Allow it to heat for at least 45 minutes.

On a lightly floured surface, stretch or roll the dough into a 12-inch round. Flour a pizza peel and transfer the round to the peel, or use a sheet of parchment paper. Top the dough with the provolone, *fior di latte*, pickles, and mortadella. Drizzle with olive oil and season with pepper.

Slide the pizza onto the preheated stone or steel and bake for 6 to 8 minutes, until the crust is puffed and golden and the cheese is bubbling.

Meanwhile, to make the ranch, in a small bowl, whisk together all the ingredients until smooth. Refrigerate until ready to use.

Remove the pizza from the oven and drizzle with the spicy ranch. Garnish with fresh basil or herbs and serve immediately.

70 Percent Hydration Pizza Dough

Makes 4 dough balls (about 250 grams each)

½ teaspoon (2 grams) active dry yeast

3 cups (700 grams) lukewarm water, divided

7¾ cups (1,000 grams) bread flour or 00 flour

2 teaspoons (10 grams) extra-virgin olive oil

4¾ teaspoons (25 grams) kosher salt

In a small bowl, dissolve the yeast in ½ cup of the water. Let stand for about 10 minutes, or until frothy.

In a large bowl or the bowl of a stand mixer fitted with the dough hook attachment, combine the flour, yeast mixture, remaining 2½ cups water, and olive oil. Mix until a shaggy dough forms. Add the salt and knead for 8 to 10 minutes in a stand mixer or 15 minutes by hand, until smooth and elastic. The dough will be soft and slightly sticky; avoid adding excess flour.

Lightly oil a large bowl and transfer the dough to the bowl. Cover and let rise at room temperature for 1½ to 2 hours, until nearly doubled in size.

Oil 4 containers or dough trays. Divide the dough into 4 equal pieces and place each piece into the container or dough tray. Cover and refrigerate for 24 to 72 hours to develop flavor and structure.

Remove the dough from the refrigerator 1 to 2 hours before baking. Gently shape as desired and bake on a preheated pizza stone or steel at 500°F to 550°F.

THE GRILL DADS' WORLD-FAMOUS PICKLE-BRINED SUCCULENT SPATCHCOCK SMOKED CHICKEN WITH A CURIOUS AND TANGY WHITE-HOT PICKLE BBQ SAUCE

MARK ANDERSON AND RYAN FEY (AKA THE GRILL DADS)

Serves 4 to 6

Mark Anderson and Ryan Fey, known collectively as The Grill Dads, aren't just backyard enthusiasts—they're serious pitmasters with decades of experience mastering fire, smoke, and flavor. Their world-famous pickle-brined spatchcocked chicken has juicy meat and perfectly crispy skin, elevated by a bold white-hot pickle BBQ sauce. Brining in dill pickle juice, buttermilk, and aromatics seasons and tenderizes the meat, while a balanced spice rub adds depth. Finishing over high heat locks in crispiness and flavor, proving why The Grill Dads are true masters of smoke and fire.

Chicken

- 1 (3½ to 5-pound) whole air-chilled organic chicken
- 1 tablespoon neutral oil

Brine

- 1 cup Kosher Dill pickle brine
- 2 tablespoons kosher salt
- 1 tablespoon granulated sugar
- 6 garlic cloves, peeled and smashed
- 2 teaspoons black peppercorns
- 2 teaspoons mustard seeds
- 1 bay leaf
- Zest of 1 lemon
- 2 cups water
- 2 cups buttermilk

Seasoning Rub

- 1 tablespoon garlic powder
- 1 tablespoon onion powder
- 1 tablespoon paprika
- 1 tablespoon light brown sugar
- 1 teaspoon ancho chili powder
- 1 teaspoon black pepper
- ½ teaspoon cayenne pepper

White-Hot Pickle BBQ Sauce

- ¼ cup finely chopped Spicy Honey Mustard pickle chips, plus more for serving
- ¼ cup Classic Dill pickle brine
- 2 cups mayonnaise
- ¼ cup apple cider vinegar
- ¼ cup prepared horseradish
- 1 tablespoon Dijon mustard
- 2 tablespoons freshly squeezed lemon juice
- 1 teaspoon garlic powder
- 1 teaspoon Worcestershire sauce
- Dash of hot sauce (such as Tapatío)
- Dash of cayenne pepper
- Kosher salt and freshly ground black pepper

To prepare the chicken, place the chicken breast side down on a cutting board. Using kitchen shears, cut along both sides of the backbone and remove it. Save the backbone to make stock later. Flip the chicken over and press firmly on the breastbone to flatten. Refrigerate until ready to brine.

To make the brine, in a large pot, combine all the ingredients except the buttermilk. Bring to a simmer over medium-high heat and cook for 20 to 30 minutes. Remove from the heat, cover, and let stand at room temperature for 1 to 2 hours. Refrigerate until fully cooled.

Stir the buttermilk into the cooled brine. Place the chicken in a large resealable plastic bag or container and pour in the brine. Seal and refrigerate for 4 to 6 hours.

Set a wire rack over a baking sheet. Remove the chicken from the brine and pat dry with paper towels. Discard the brine. Place the chicken on the wire rack. For crispier skin, refrigerate uncovered for up to 4 hours.

To make the seasoning rub, in a small bowl, stir together all the ingredients. Rub the chicken lightly with the oil, then sprinkle the rub evenly over the entire surface, coating all sides thoroughly.

Preheat a smoker or grill to 275°F. Place the chicken skin-side up directly on the grates. Smoke for 1½ to 2 hours, until the internal temperature of the thickest part of the breast reaches 160°F and the thigh registers about 175°F. Use an instant-read thermometer for best results.

Transfer the chicken to a platter and let rest for 15 minutes. Meanwhile, increase the grill temperature to 400°F. Return the chicken to the grill for 3 to 5 minutes to crisp the skin.

continued

While the chicken is smoking, prepare the sauce. In a medium bowl, whisk together all the ingredients until smooth. Season to taste with salt and pepper. Cover and refrigerate for at least 30 minutes before serving.

Slice the rested chicken and serve with the sauce on the side or brushed over the top. Garnish and serve with additional pickles, along with your favorite barbecue sides.

PICKLE-BRINED FRIED CHICKEN

Serves 4 to 6

Pickle brine isn't just for flavor—it changes the chicken on a molecular level. The salt in the brine helps proteins unwind and retain more water, which means the meat stays juicy even after frying. Acids in the brine lightly break down the meat, making each bite more tender. In this recipe, thighs get an extra boost from buttermilk, then a dredge in spiced flour that fries up into golden, craggy crunch. The result: crispy outside, impossibly moist inside.

Brine

½ cup Jalapeño pickle brine
¼ cup buttermilk
1 teaspoon kosher salt
2 pounds boneless, skinless chicken thighs

Breading

2 cups all-purpose flour
¼ cup cornstarch
1 tablespoon kosher salt
2 teaspoons black pepper
2 teaspoons smoked paprika
1 teaspoon garlic powder
1 teaspoon onion powder
1 teaspoon cayenne pepper
½ teaspoon baking powder
2 tablespoons pickle brine
Vegetable oil, for frying

To make the brine, in a large bowl, whisk together the pickle brine, buttermilk, and salt. Add the chicken thighs, ensuring they are fully submerged. Cover and refrigerate for at least 4 hours or up to overnight.

To make the breading, in a shallow dish, whisk together the flour, cornstarch, salt, pepper, paprika, garlic powder, onion powder, cayenne pepper, and baking powder. Add the brine and mix it in with your hands until the mixture forms small clumps, resembling coarse crumbs.

Remove the chicken from the brine, letting the excess liquid drip off. Discard the brine. Dredge each piece in the breading mixture, pressing gently to ensure a thick, even coating. Transfer to a wire rack and let rest for 15 minutes. Set a clean wire rack over a baking dish.

In a large, heavy-bottomed pot or deep skillet, heat 1½ inches of vegetable oil to 350°F. Working in batches, fry the chicken for 5 to 7 minutes, turning occasionally, until golden brown and the internal temperature reaches 165°F.

Transfer the chicken to the clean wire rack to drain. Let rest briefly before serving.

SRIRACHA SAUERKRAUT FRIED RICE

Serves 4

I make this fried rice when I want a quick and hearty meal. The sriracha sauerkraut gives this dish an interesting dimension, and a splash of sauerkraut brine helps everything soak in those flavors. I toss in whatever protein I have on hand—chicken, shrimp, or bacon—and fold in scrambled eggs at the end, as with any good fried rice!

3 tablespoons extra-virgin olive oil

Meat of choice: 1 chicken breast, cubed, or 4 slices thick-cut bacon, chopped, or 8–10 medium shrimp (41/50 count), tails removed

4 green onions, white and green parts, chopped

3 assorted bell peppers, seeded and medium diced

3 tablespoons oyster sauce

¼ cup soy sauce or tamari

2 garlic cloves, peeled and roughly chopped

2 tablespoons sambal oelek

½ cup sriracha sauerkraut

2 cups cooked jasmine rice

2 tablespoons sauerkraut brine

3 eggs

Heat a wok or large, deep skillet over medium-high heat. Add the olive oil and heat until shimmering.

Add your protein of choice and cook through. Remove from the pan and set aside.

Add the green onion to the same pan along with the bell pepper, oyster sauce, soy sauce, garlic, and sambal oelek to the pan. Cook for 5 minutes, stirring often.

Add the sauerkraut, cooked protein, rice, and brine. Stir to combine and cook for 5 more minutes.

Push the rice to the sides of the pan to make a space in the center. Scramble the eggs directly in that spot, then fold them into the rice mixture. Serve warm.

Clockwise from top left: Creamy Sweet Heat Corn (pg. 64), Pickle-Brined Stuffed Pork Loin Roulade (pg. 115), Warm Honey Mustard Smashed Potato Salad (pg. 73)

PICKLE-BRINED STUFFED PORK LOIN ROULADE

Serves 6 to 8

Soaking the pork loin in pickle brine before roasting does more than add flavor—it helps the meat stay juicy and tender. Once brined, the loin is rolled around a filling of spinach, feta, and sun-dried tomatoes, then roasted to perfection. Serve it as a centerpiece for dinner, and if there are leftovers (emphasis on "if"), slice it thin for sandwiches.

3 pounds pork loin

1¼ cups pickle brine

2 tablespoons extra-virgin olive oil, divided

Kosher salt and freshly ground black pepper

1 Horseradish pickle

1 cup sun-dried tomatoes

¼ cup olive tapenade

1 (6-ounce) bag fresh spinach, steamed and cooled

¼ cup crumbled feta cheese

10 garlic cloves, peeled

⅓ cup unsalted butter, at room temperature

1 tablespoon brown sugar

1 tablespoon smoked paprika

Place the pork loin flat on a large cutting board. Using a sharp knife, carefully butterfly the loin by slicing it lengthwise without cutting all the way through, so it opens like a book.

Transfer the pork loin to a shallow baking dish and pour the brine over the meat. Cover and refrigerate for at least 3 hours or up to overnight, turning occasionally.

Drain and discard the brine. Pat the pork dry and rub both sides with 1 tablespoon of the olive oil. Season with salt and pepper.

In a food processor, combine the pickle, sun-dried tomatoes, tapenade, spinach, feta, and garlic. Pulse until well combined.

Spread the filling along the center of the pork loin, leaving a ½-inch border on all sides. Roll the loin tightly into a log, seam-side down. Using kitchen twine, tie the roulade securely every 2 inches.

In a small bowl, whisk together the butter, brown sugar, and paprika. Brush the mixture evenly over the top of the roulade.

continued

Preheat the oven to 450°F. Line a baking sheet with parchment paper and place a wire rack on top. Place the pork roulade on the wire rack and roast for 15 minutes. Decrease the oven temperature to 325°F and continue roasting for about 1 hour and 5 minutes, or until the internal temperature reaches 145°F.

Remove from the oven and let rest for 10 minutes. Snip and discard the kitchen twine. Slice the pork into ½-inch-thick rounds and serve.

SWEETS

Pickles in dessert might sound unexpected—but the balance of sweet, salty, and acidic is exactly what makes these recipes work. I use brine and bold flavor to create contrast, cut through richness, and bring something new to the table.

From frozen Pickle Popsicles (page 119) and Bread and Butter Pickle Sherbet Sundae (page 126) to Cashew Brittle (page 120), Pickle Lemon Bars (page 123), and Apple and Bread and Butter Pickle Crumble (page 124), these desserts are built on the idea that acidity and crunch can elevate sweets just as much as sugar and butter do. A little zip sharpens the flavor and brings a sense of adventure to lovable confections. You don't have to be a die-hard pickle lover to enjoy these recipes—but you *will* appreciate the pickley interplay of your after-dinner cravings.

PICKLE POPSICLES

Makes 6

Are you excited about frozen pickle juice? You should be, because these Popsicles are downright addictive. They're salty, cool, and thirst quenching—a snack that keeps you reaching back for more, whether you're lounging in the sun or just need a moment of frozen relief.

1½ cups pickle brine

2 tablespoons granulated sugar

12 pickle chips (such as Spicy Dill or Bread and Butter)

In a pitcher, combine the brine and sugar. Stir until the sugar is fully dissolved.

Pour the mixture into six Popsicle molds. Add 2 pickle chips to each mold, then insert the Popsicle sticks and cover.

Freeze for at least 6 hours or overnight, until solid.

To release the Popsicles, run the molds briefly under warm water. Serve immediately.

VARIATION: For an adult version, add a splash of vodka or whiskey before freezing.

CASHEW BRITTLE

Makes 12 to 16 pieces

This isn't your standard peanut brittle—though it starts like one with sugar and corn syrup, it takes a savory detour thanks to dill pickle brine and cashews. The brine keeps the candy glossy and adds subtle seasoning, while the Dill Pickle Cashews and freeze-dried pickles give texture and bursts of pickle flavor that sneak up on you. Warning: the sugar gets extremely hot, so handle with care while stirring and pouring! Use caution when working over the stove and handling the brittle mixture.

Neutral oil, for greasing spatula

1 cup granulated sugar

½ cup light corn syrup

¼ cup dill pickle brine, strained

2 tablespoons unsalted butter

1 cup Dill-Pickled Cashews (page 49)

1 teaspoon vanilla extract

½ teaspoon baking soda

½ ounce freeze-dried pickles, pulsed in a food processor until crumbly

Line a baking sheet with parchment paper or a silicone baking mat. Lightly oil a heatproof spatula and set aside.

In a medium saucepan over medium heat, combine the sugar, corn syrup, and brine. Stir to combine, then let the mixture come to a boil without stirring. Clip a candy thermometer to the side of the pot. When the mixture reaches 270°F (soft crack stage), carefully stir in the butter and cashews. Continue cooking, stirring frequently, until the mixture reaches 300°F (hard crack stage).

Remove from the heat. Quickly stir in the vanilla and baking soda—the mixture will foam. Immediately pour the brittle onto the prepared baking sheet and spread evenly with the oiled spatula. Sprinkle the crushed freeze-dried pickles evenly over the surface.

Let cool completely, 30 to 60 minutes. Break into pieces and store in an airtight container at room temperature for up to 2 weeks.

APPLE AND BREAD AND BUTTER PICKLE CRUMBLE

Makes 1 (8-inch) crumble

This dish feels right at home on a summer picnic table or a Thanksgiving dessert spread. Tart apples meet the sweet-sour snap of Bread and Butter pickles, creating a filling that's both familiar and a little daring. On top, a golden oat crumble bakes into a warm, toasty blanket that makes every spoonful exciting.

Filling

- 2 pounds medium Granny Smith apples (about 5 to 6), cored and medium diced
- ½ cup finely chopped Bread and Butter pickle chips
- ¼ cup Bread and Butter pickle brine
- ¼ cup packed dark brown sugar
- 1 teaspoon ground cinnamon
- ½ teaspoon ground nutmeg
- 2 tablespoons cornstarch

Crumble Topping

- ¾ cup rolled oats
- ½ cup all-purpose flour
- ½ cup packed dark brown sugar
- ¼ teaspoon kosher salt
- ½ teaspoon ground cinnamon
- ½ teaspoon ground nutmeg
- ½ cup (1 stick) cold unsalted butter, cut into cubes
- 1 tablespoon strained Bread and Butter pickle brine
- Bread and Butter Pickle Sherbet (page 126), for serving

Preheat the oven to 350°F. Lightly butter an 8-inch pie pan.

To make the filling, in a large bowl, combine all the ingredients. Toss until the apples are well coated. Spread the mixture evenly in the prepared pan.

To make the crumble topping, in a separate, medium bowl, stir together the oats, flour, brown sugar, salt, cinnamon, and nutmeg. Add the butter and the brine. Using a fork or your fingers, work the butter into the mixture until it forms coarse crumbs.

Sprinkle the topping evenly over the apple filling. Bake for 35 to 40 minutes, until the topping is golden brown and the filling is bubbling. Let cool slightly before serving. Serve warm, ideally with the pickle sherbet.

BREAD AND BUTTER PICKLE SHERBET SUNDAE

I know it sounds wild, and it *is wild*, but trust me—this sundae is worth every raised eyebrow. Sweet, creamy pickle sherbet gets scooped into a hollowed dill pickle. Yes, you read that right. No bananas in this sundae. Then it goes all out with Mexican candies for a flavor explosion that's part sweet and part salty. It's creamy, it's chewy, it'll make you blush.

Bread and Butter Pickle Sherbet

Makes about 1 quart

1 cup Bread and Butter pickle brine

1 cup Bread and Butter pickle chips

1 (14-ounce) can sweetened condensed milk

2 tablespoons apple cider vinegar

¼ teaspoon ground turmeric

¼ teaspoon ground cinnamon

¼ teaspoon Dijon mustard

6 drops green food coloring (optional)

Sundae

2 scoops Bread and Butter Pickle Sherbet

1 large dill pickle, hollowed out

Mexican candies (such as chamoy, Lucas powder, fruit roll-ups, or other pickle-flavored varieties)

To make the sherbet, in a blender, combine all the ingredients. Blend until very smooth.

Transfer the mixture to a container and refrigerate for at least 1 hour, until well chilled.

Churn in an ice cream maker according to the manufacturer's instructions, until thick and creamy. Transfer to a freezer-safe container and freeze for at least 4 hours or overnight, until firm.

To assemble the sundae, place 2 scoops sherbet into the pickle. Top with your favorite Mexican pickle-flavored candies and sauces. Serve immediately.

COCKTAILS

I'm bringing the brine to your coupes with cocktails that are salty, spicy, and totally unexpected.

Starting with the OG Pickleback Shot (page 134), of course (I mean, this is kind of expected), but with a twist. Think frozen hollowed-out pickles turned into shot glasses. Once you've reached peak buzz, shake (or stir) an ice-cold K+K Street Dirty Martini (page 131), a Jalapeño Pickle Margarita (page 135), and a Pickled Bourbon Sour (page 143) that might just ruin all others for you.

These drinks use brine the same way great bartenders use citrus or bitters—to sharpen, balance, and bring depth. Whether you're making one for yourself or a whole flight for friends, one thing's certain: it's brine o'clock somewhere.

BLOODY MARY

Serves 1

The Bloody Mary is a brunch must for good reason—it's savory, satiating, and endlessly customizable. This version leans on Horseradish pickle brine for a kick that cuts through the richness of tomato juice and vodka. Perfect for a slow Sunday morning or "hair of the dog," when the night before got a little too fun with other pickle drinks.

6 to 8 ounces chilled tomato juice

1 ounce freshly squeezed lemon juice

2 teaspoons Worcestershire sauce

1 ounce Horseradish pickle brine (shake before using)

½ teaspoon Tabasco hot sauce

½ teaspoon celery salt

⅛ teaspoon black pepper

1½ to 2 ounces chilled vodka

Pickle of choice or celery, for garnish

In a cocktail shaker, combine the tomato juice, lemon juice, Worcestershire sauce, brine, hot sauce, celery salt, pepper, and vodka. Fill with ice and shake vigorously.

Fill a pint or Collins glass with ice. Strain the drink into the glass, garnish, and serve.

PICKLES

K+K STREET DIRTY MARTINI

Serves 1

If you like your martini extra dirty, this one doesn't hold back. In fact, I call it "street dirty" because you can't see through the glass! Olive juice provides the classic salinity, while pickle brine adds sharper acidity and a touch of heat that olive juice alone can't deliver. This recipe uses Jalapeño pickle brine for a fiery kick, but if you prefer your dirty without the spice, swap in regular pickle brine. Either way, this martini is unruly!

Ice
2½ ounces vodka or gin
1¼ ounces Jalapeño pickle brine
1¼ ounces green olive juice
Pickle spear or pickle chips, for garnish

Chill a coupe glass. Fill a cocktail shaker with ice and add the vodka, brine, and olive juice. Shake vigorously for 15 to 20 seconds.

Strain into the glass, garnish, and serve.

FROZEN PICKLE SHOT

Makes 2 shots (or more, depending on quantity made)

Why settle for a plain shot glass when the pickle can do the job itself, giving you both a snack and a drink all in one? These frozen dill pickle "glasses" not only hold your liquor but also chill it to the bone. It's so good and so fun, especially since there isn't any cleanup!

1 large Classic Dill or Jalapeño pickle

Alcohol of choice (such as vodka, tequila, or whiskey)

Cut the pickle in half crosswise. Slice a thin piece off the rounded end of each half so it can stand upright.

Using a small spoon, melon baller, or paring knife, carefully hollow out most of the interior, leaving enough at the bottom and sides to hold liquid. Reserve the scooped-out pickle flesh.

Repeat with additional pickles as desired.

Place the hollowed pickle halves upright in a freezer-safe container, such as an open lidded container or small dish. Freeze for 2 to 3 hours, until firm.

Fill the frozen pickle "shot glasses" with your alcohol of choice and serve immediately. Alternatively, fill them before freezing for an ultra-chilled experience. Serve immediately. Take the shot, then take a bite of the pickle.

Freeze the scooped pickle flesh in an ice cube tray with a bit of brine to make pickle cubes for later use.

OG PICKLEBACK SHOT

Serves 1

This is the classic shot of whiskey chased with pickle brine. It's the kind of bar ritual that gets you great memories—or in trouble.

1 ounce whiskey (any variety)
1 ounce pickle brine

Pour the whiskey into a shot glass and the brine into a separate shot glass.

Take the whiskey shot, then immediately follow with the brine shot to mellow the flavor.

JALAPEÑO PICKLE MARGARITA

Serves 1

I love margaritas because you can make them a million different ways, and this one is my favorite for when I want something with a kick. I use Jalapeño pickle brine because spicy margaritas are my favorite, but it also plays so well with the tequila and lime. The salted rim (always optional) makes every sip even more satisfying. A pickle slice on top is my little signature touch.

Salt, for rimming the glass

1 ounce freshly squeezed lime juice

Ice

2 ounces tequila

1 ounce Jalapeño pickle brine

Pickled jalapeño slices

Pickle slice or jalapeño slice, for garnish

Place salt on a plate. Rim a rocks glass with a lime wedge, then dip into the salt to coat. Fill with ice.

Fill a cocktail shaker with ice and add the tequila, lime juice, brine, and a few pickled jalapeño slices (to your taste). Shake and strain into the glass, garnish, and serve.

MANGO MEZCALITA

RANDY TARLOW OF LIQUID ALCHEMIST

Serves 1

Randy Tarlow, the founder of Liquid Alchemist and a cocktail industry veteran, loves mezcal, and so do I, so it's a thrill to have it paired with pickles for this book. Mezcal has a distinctive smoky and earthy character that gives it its acquired taste. But shaken with mango syrup and Jalapeño pickle brine, it's one of those drinks you sip and say, "Uh-oh, this one is dangerous."

Kosher salt, for rimming the glass
Tajin spice, for rimming the glass
1 ounce lime juice, plus more for rimming the glass
2 ounces mezcal
½ ounce premium orange liqueur
1½ ounces Liquid Alchemist mango syrup
¼ ounce Jalapeño pickle brine
Ice
2 thin mango slices, for garnish

Combine the salt and Tajín on a plate. Rim a rocks glass with a lime wedge, then dip into the spices to coat. Fill with ice.

Fill a cocktail shaker with ice and add all the ingredients. Shake and strain into the glass, garnish, and serve.

SUMMER SOLSTICE

TONY ABOU-GANIM

Serves 1

When it comes to cocktails, Tony Abou-Ganim—who has been influential in shaping modern mixology—knows how to make a drink worth remembering. This martini riff takes the elegance of a martini and gives it a garden-fresh twist. Tomato water—infused with pickle brine, basil, and cucumber—adds a clean, savory backbone that pairs beautifully with chilled vodka. A few drops of olive oil and fresh basil on top give it a refined finish. For a spicier version, infuse the vodka with a combination of fresh chile peppers.

Cocktail

Ice

2½ ounces Tito's vodka

½ ounce Tomato Water (recipe below)

3 drops extra-virgin olive oil, for garnish

Fresh basil sprig, for garnish

Sweet Heat pickle chips, for serving

Tomato Water

Makes about 1 cup

3 ounces K + K Sweet Heat pickle brine

2 pounds very ripe tomatoes (such as Early Girl, Valencia, or beefsteak)

½ cup fresh basil leaves

½ cup fresh cilantro leaves (optional)

1 cucumber, peeled and diced

Pinch of sea salt

To make the tomato water, line a fine-mesh sieve with a double layer of cheesecloth and set it over a large bowl.

In a food processor or blender, pulse the brine, tomatoes, basil, cilantro, if using, cucumber, and salt until coarsely chopped.

Transfer the mixture to the prepared sieve. Refrigerate and allow to strain undisturbed for 12 hours. Do not stir or press the solids or the Tomato Water will become cloudy. Discard the solids. Bottle the Tomato Water and refrigerate for up to 3 days.

To make the cocktail, freeze a cocktail coupe. Fill a mixing beaker with ice and add the vodka and the Tomato Water. Stir until well chilled.

Strain into the coupe and garnish. Serve with a side of K + K Sweet Heat pickle chips.

DUST BOWL PUNCH

RANDY TARLOW OF LIQUID ALCHEMIST

Serves 1

Randy Tarlow created Dust Bowl Punch to capture both history and flavor. Bread and butter pickles, first trademarked by Omar and Cora Fanning in the early 1920s, earned their name because jars were often traded for staples like bread and butter. During the Dust Bowl, families relied on these sweet-and-sour preserves to stretch limited resources and add flavor when fresh produce was scarce. In this cocktail, pickle brine adds a nod to that ingenuity, brightening rye, ginger, and honey with a subtle historic twist.

Ice

2 ounces rye whiskey

½ ounce Bread and Butter pickle brine

1 ounce freshly squeezed lemon juice

1 ounce Liquid Alchemist ginger syrup

¼ ounce honey syrup (see note)

2 dashes Angostura bitters

Candied ginger, for garnish

Bread and Butter pickle chip, for garnish

Chill a rocks glass. Fill a cocktail shaker with ice and add the whiskey, brine, lemon juice, ginger syrup, honey syrup, and bitters. Shake until well chilled. Fill the glass with ice and strain the cocktail into the glass. Garnish with skewered candied ginger or a Bread and Butter pickle chip.

NOTE: To make honey syrup, combine equal parts honey and warm water. Stir until fully dissolved.

PICKLED COLLINS

Serves 1

I've always enjoyed a classic Collins for its crisp, effervescent simplicity, but I like to use pickle-infused vodka for a savory note that makes each sip more intriguing. Lemon juice and simple syrup keep it bright and refreshing, and topped with bubbly club soda, this is my go-to cocktail when I want something light but full of flavor.

2 ounces pickle-infused vodka
1 ounce freshly squeezed lemon juice
1 ounce simple syrup
Ice
Club soda
Pickle slice, for garnish
Lemon wheel, for garnish

In a shaker, combine the vodka, lemon juice, and simple syrup. Fill with ice and shake well. Fill a Collins glass with ice and strain the cocktail into the glass. Top with club soda and stir gently. Garnish and serve.

PICKLED BOURBON SOUR

Serves 1

When I want a cocktail that's bold but balanced, I reach for my Pickled Bourbon Sour. I love how the pickle brine adds a sharpness that plays off the rich bourbon, while lemon juice and a touch of simple syrup keep everything just so perfectly balanced. This drink is incredibly refreshing year-round.

Ice
2 ounces bourbon
1 ounce pickle brine
1 ounce freshly squeezed lemon juice
½ ounce simple syrup
Pickle slice, for garnish

Fill a cocktail shaker with ice and add the bourbon, brine, lemon juice, and simple syrup. Shake well until chilled. Chill a coupe or fill a rocks glass with ice and strain the cocktail into the glass. Garnish and serve.

PICKLE ASTROLOGY SIGNS

WHAT KIND OF PICKLE ARE YOU BASED ON YOUR ZODIAC SIGN?

Capricorn (December 22–January 19): Whole Pickle

Classic, sturdy, and all business—Capricorns don't mess around, and neither does a whole pickle. No frills, no nonsense, just straight-up crunch and flavor.

Aquarius (January 20–February 18): Pickle Relish

Unique, unconventional, and adding unexpected flair to anything—Aquarius is the pickle relish of the zodiac. They're adaptable, always shaking things up, and never boring.

Pisces (February 19–March 20): Pickle Juice

Dreamy, emotional, and a little misunderstood—Pisces is the essence of the pickle, just like pickle juice. Some people don't get it, but those who do can't live without it.

Aries (March 21–April 19): Spicy Pickle

Bold, fiery, and impossible to ignore—just like Aries. Spicy pickles bring the heat and excitement to any meal, much like Aries lights up any room they walk into.

Taurus (April 20–May 20): Bread and Butter Pickle

Reliable, comforting, and a little bit sweet—Taurus loves the finer things in life, and Bread and Butter pickles are the perfect balance of indulgence and tradition.

Gemini (May 21–June 20): Half-Sour Pickle

Always in between two worlds, Gemini thrives on contrast. Half-sour pickles are crisp, fresh, and still partly a cucumber—just like Gemini, they refuse to be one thing or the other.

Cancer (June 21–July 22): Classic Dill Pickle

Nostalgic, dependable, and a household staple—just like Cancer. Dill pickles bring comfort, and there's nothing more reassuring than that familiar crunch.

Leo (July 23–August 22): Kosher Dill Pickle

Bold, flavorful, and a little extra—Leos love the spotlight, and Kosher Dills bring that extra punch of garlic and zest. They're not just pickles; they're *the* pickles.

Virgo (August 23–September 22): Gherkin

Small but mighty, gherkins are precise, refined, and always put together—just like Virgo. They may not be flashy, but they're essential in the right setting.

Libra (September 23–October 22): Sweet Pickle

Libras are charming and diplomatic and have a naturally sweet personality—so of course they'd be sweet pickles! A little sassy but mostly lovable, they keep the balance just right.

Scorpio (October 23–November 21): Sour Pickle

Intense, mysterious, and with a bite that lingers—Scorpios don't do mild, and neither do sour pickles. They take their time to develop, but once they're ready, they're unforgettable.

Sagittarius (November 22–December 21): Cornichon

Adventurous and worldly, Sagittarius needs a pickle with international flair. French cornichons are tiny but pack a sharp, vinegary punch—perfect for a sign that's always seeking something bold.

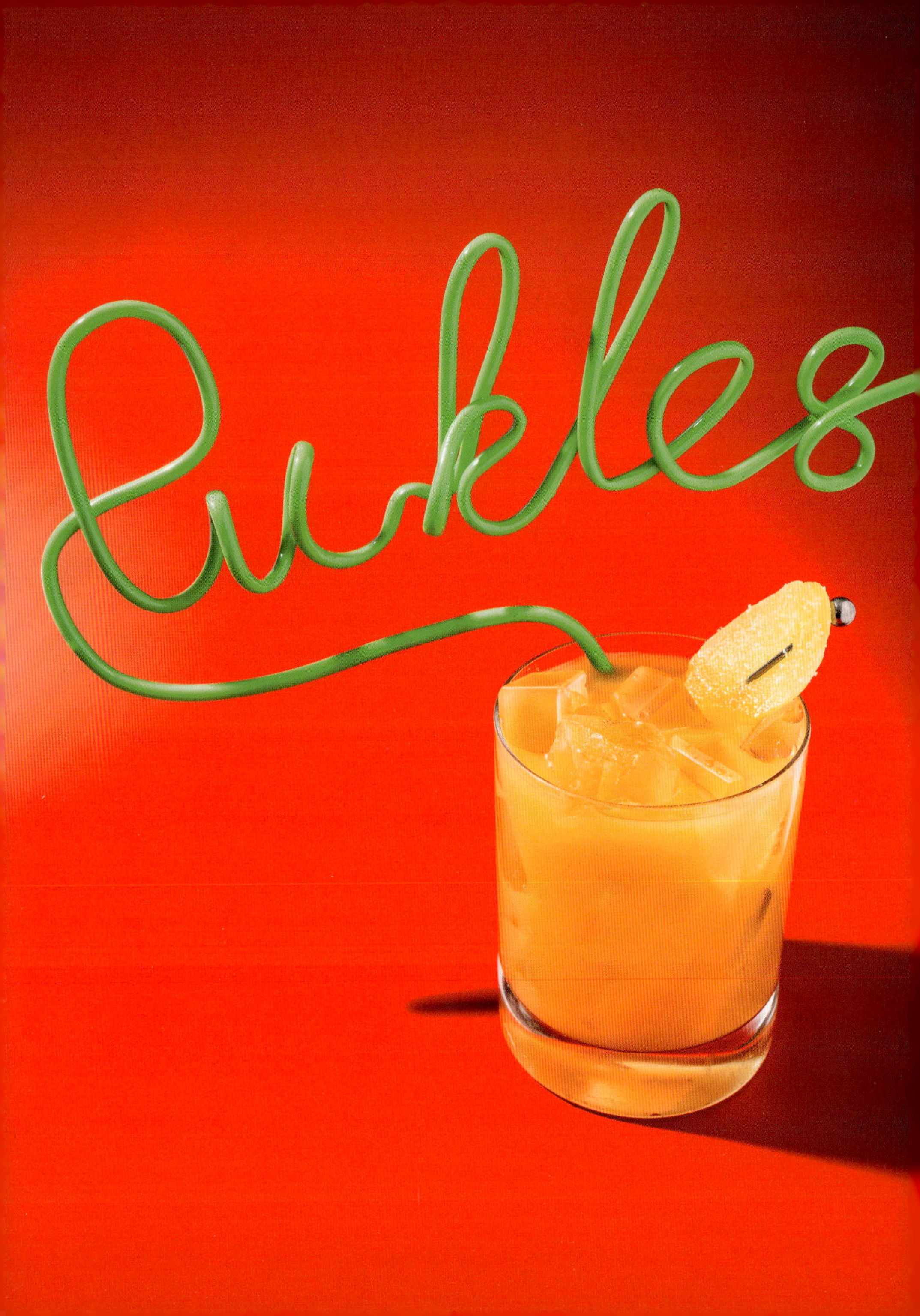

ACKNOWLEDGMENTS

Creating this cookbook has been a journey filled with flavor, memories, and collaboration, and I am deeply grateful to those who helped bring it to life.

First and foremost, I want to thank my family: my wife, Helena; my daughters, Alli and Jessi; my sons-in-law, Sean and Bar; my sister, Roni, who created the artwork for the cover, pickle evolution, and astrology; and my niece, Alix. Your unwavering support, honest feedback, and shared love of food have been the heart of this project.

To the contributors—J. B. Smoove for the foreword and the wonderful recipes from Cat Cora, Joy Bauer, Chef Daniele Uditi of Pizzana, Mark Anderson and Ryan Fey (aka The Grill Dads), Lady and Larder, Chris Abouabdo of Foodbeast, Randy Tarlow, and Tony Abou-Ganim—thank you for generously sharing your time, recipes, and culinary wisdom. Your passion and creativity have added richness and depth to these pages, and this book would not be the same without your input.

To my Team—Tiffany Senin, Danielle Bernabe, and Eddie Sanchez—it is hard to find words to truly express how beyond grateful I am. Your support, creativity, and unwavering drive to get this across the finish line are unmatched.

Together, you have all helped turn an idea into something I'm proud to share with the world. For the love of pickles belongs to all of us!!!

With heartfelt thanks,

METRIC EQUIVALENTS AND CONVERSIONS

APPROXIMATE METRIC EQUIVALENTS

Volume

¼ teaspoon	1 milliliter
½ teaspoon	2.5 milliliters
¾ teaspoon	4 milliliters
1 teaspoon	5 milliliters
1¼ teaspoons	6 milliliters
1½ teaspoons	7.5 milliliters
1¾ teaspoons	8.5 milliliters
2 teaspoons	10 milliliters
1 tablespoon (½ fluid ounce)	15 milliliters
2 tablespoons (1 fluid ounce)	30 milliliters
¼ cup	60 milliliters
⅓ cup	80 milliliters
½ cup (4 fluid ounces)	120 milliliters
⅔ cup	160 milliliters
¾ cup	180 milliliters
1 cup (8 fluid ounces)	240 milliliters
1¼ cups	300 milliliters
1½ cups (12 fluid ounces)	360 milliliters
1⅔ cups	400 milliliters
2 cups (1 pint)	480 milliliters
3 cups	720 milliliters
4 cups (1 quart)	0.96 liter
1 quart plus ¼ cup	1 liter
4 quarts (1 gallon)	3.8 liters

Mass

¼ ounce	7 grams
½ ounce	14 grams
¾ ounce	21 grams
1 ounce	28 grams
1¼ ounces	35 grams
1½ ounces	42.5 grams
1⅔ ounces	47 grams
2 ounces	57 grams
3 ounces	85 grams
4 ounces (¼ pound)	113 grams
5 ounces	142 grams
6 ounces	170 grams
7 ounces	198 grams
8 ounces (½ pound)	227 grams
16 ounces (1 pound)	454 grams
35.25 ounces (2.2 pounds)	1 kilogram

Length

⅛ inch	3 millimeters
¼ inch	6.25 millimeters
½ inch	1.25 centimeters
1 inch	2.5 centimeters
2 inches	5 centimeters
2½ inches	6.25 centimeters
4 inches	10 centimeters
5 inches	12.75 centimeters
6 inches	15.25 centimeters
12 inches (1 foot)	30.5 centimeters

COMMON INGREDIENTS & THEIR APPROXIMATE EQUIVALENTS

1 cup uncooked white rice = 185 grams
1 cup all-purpose flour = 120 grams
1 stick butter (4 ounces • ½ cup • 8 tablespoons) = 110 grams
1 cup butter (8 ounces • 2 sticks • 16 tablespoons) = 220 grams
1 cup brown sugar, firmly packed = 213 grams
1 cup granulated sugar = 200 grams

OVEN TEMPERATURES

To convert Fahrenheit to Celsius, subtract 32 from Fahrenheit, multiply the result by 5, then divide by 9.

Description	Fahrenheit	Celsius	British Gas Mark
Very cool	200°	95°	0
Very cool	225°	110°	¼
Very cool	250°	120°	½
Cool	275°	135°	1
Cool	300°	150°	2
Warm	325°	165°	3
Moderate	350°	175°	4
Moderately hot	375°	190°	5
Fairly hot	400°	200°	6
Hot	425°	220°	7
Very hot	450°	230°	8
Very hot	475°	245°	9

METRIC CONVERSION FORMULAS

To Convert	Multiply
Ounces to grams	Ounces by 28.35
Pounds to kilograms	Pounds by .454
Teaspoons to milliliters	Teaspoons by 4.93
Tablespoons to milliliters	Tablespoons by 14.79
Fluid ounces to milliliters	Fluid ounces by 29.57
Cups to milliliters	Cups by 240
Cups to liters	Cups by .236
Pints to liters	Pints by .473
Quarts to liters	Quarts by .946
Gallons to liters	Gallons by 3.785
Inches to centimeters	Inches by 2.54

Information compiled from a variety of sources, including *Recipes Into Type* by Joan Whitman and Dolores Simon (Newton, MA: Biscuit Books, 1993); *The New Food Lover's Companion* by Sharon Tyler Herbst (Hauppauge, NY: Barron's, 2013); and *Rosemary Brown's Big Kitchen Instruction Book* (Kansas City, MO: Andrews McMeel, 1998).

BIBLIOGRAPHY

Britannica Editors. "Cucumber." Encyclopedia Britannica, October 7, 2025. https://www.britannica.com/plant/cucumber.

State Historical Society of North Dakota. (n.d.). *Section 1: Scurvy in the Frontier Army* [Unit 3: Set 6: Gardens at Frontier Military Posts 1864–1880]. Retrieved from https://www.history.nd.gov/textbook/unit3_comculcon/unit3_6_1_intro.html?utm_source=chatgpt.com.

Terebelski, D., & Ralph, N. (2003). *Pickle History Timeline*. NY Food Museum. http://www.nyfoodmuseum.org/_ptime.htm.

Younkin, R. (2019). *Pickling: It's Not Just for Cucumbers* [PDF]. Montana State University Extension. https://apps.msuextension.org/magazine/assets/docs/PicklingVarieties.pdf?utm_source=chatgpt.com.

FOR THE LOVE OF PICKLES

The authorised representative in the EEA is Simon and Schuster Netherlands BV,
Herculesplein 96 3584 AA Utrecht, Netherlands. (info@simonandschuster.nl)

Andrews McMeel Publishing
a division of Andrews McMeel Universal
1130 Walnut Street, Kansas City, Missouri 64106

www.andrewsmcmeel.com

26 27 28 29 30 TEN 10 9 8 7 6 5 4 3 2 1

ISBN: 979-8-8816-0552-0

Library of Congress Control Number: 2026930330

Editor: Jean Z. Lucas
Art Director/Designer: Holly Swayne
Production Editor: Brianna Westervelt
Production Manager: Jeff Preuss
Photography: Eddie Sanchez

FSC www.fsc.org MIX Paper | Supporting responsible forestry FSC® C016973